First World War
and Army of Occupation
War Diary
France, Belgium and Germany

41 DIVISION
Divisional Troops
Royal Army Service Corps
297 Company ASC
8 May 1916 - 31 October 1919

WO95/2631/4

The Naval & Military Press Ltd
www.nmarchive.com
Published in association with The National Archives

Published by

The Naval & Military Press Ltd

Unit 10 Ridgewood Industrial Park,

Uckfield, East Sussex,

TN22 5QE England

Tel: +44 (0) 1825 749494

www.naval-military-press.com

www.nmarchive.com

This diary has been reprinted in facsimile from the original. Any imperfections are inevitably reproduced and the quality may fall short of modern type and cartographic standards.

© **Crown Copyright**
Images reproduced by permission of The National Archives, London, England, 2015.

Contents

Document type	Place/Title	Date From	Date To
Heading	WO95/2631/4 297 Coy Asc		
Heading	BEF 41 Div Train 297 Coy ASC 1916 May-1917 Oct 1918 Mar-1919 Oct. In Italy 1917 Nov-1918 Feb.		
War Diary	Loote Boom F.10.c.6.5 Sheet 36A	08/05/1916	10/05/1916
War Diary	La Creche B.1.c.3.6 (Sheet 36)	11/05/1916	13/05/1916
War Diary	La Creche	14/05/1916	31/05/1916
War Diary	La Creche A.5.d.5.9 (Sheet 36)	01/06/1916	08/06/1916
War Diary	La Creche	09/06/1916	30/06/1916
War Diary	La Creche A.5.d.5.9. Sheet 36	01/07/1916	14/08/1916
War Diary	Caestre W.2.b.9.8 Sheet 27.	15/08/1916	24/08/1916
War Diary	Long Square (L) (6) on Map 1/100000 Abbeville 14	25/08/1916	31/08/1916
War Diary	Long Map Abbeville No. 14. 1/100,000 Square (L) (6).	01/09/1916	05/09/1916
War Diary	Argoeuves Map Amiens 17 1/100000 Square (C) (1).	06/09/1916	06/09/1916
War Diary	Buire-Sur-L'Ancre D.24.c.0.8 Sheet 62 D.	07/09/1916	10/09/1916
War Diary	Albert Sheet 62 D E.10.b.1.5.	11/09/1916	18/09/1916
War Diary	Buire-Sur L'Ancre	19/09/1916	20/09/1916
War Diary	Buire-Sur L'Ancre D.24.c.0.8 Map 62 D.	21/09/1916	02/10/1916
War Diary	Becordel-Becourt F.7.c.5.7 Sheet 62 D.	03/10/1916	11/10/1916
War Diary	Dernancourt E.15.a.3.5 Sheet 62 D.	12/10/1916	15/10/1916
War Diary	Dernancourt	16/10/1916	16/10/1916
War Diary	Argoeuves Map Amiens 17 Square (C) (1)	17/10/1916	17/10/1916
War Diary	Huchenneville Map Abbeville No Square	18/10/1916	21/10/1916
War Diary	Caestre W.2.b.9.8 Sheet 27.	22/10/1916	27/10/1916
War Diary	Reninghelst	28/10/1916	31/10/1916
War Diary	Reninghelst M.5.c.3.8 Sheet 28	01/11/1916	25/04/1917
War Diary	Beauvoorde K.34.c.5.8 Sheet 27	26/04/1917	27/04/1917
War Diary	Rubrouck H.8.c.2.2 Sheet 27	28/04/1917	28/04/1917
War Diary	Monnecove J.36.d.1.8 Sheet 27 A.	29/04/1917	15/05/1917
War Diary	Rubrouck H.8.c.2.2. Sheet 27	16/05/1917	16/05/1917
War Diary	Beauvoorde K.34.c.5.8. Sheet 27	17/05/1917	17/05/1917
War Diary	Reninghelst	18/05/1917	31/05/1917
War Diary	Reninghelst G.34.b.6.6. Sheet 28	01/06/1917	04/06/1917
War Diary	Reninghelst M.4.b.2.9. Sheet 28.	05/06/1917	14/06/1917
War Diary	Ouderdom G.36.a.3.7	15/06/1917	19/06/1917
War Diary	Reninghelst (M.5.b.8.4.)	20/06/1917	22/06/1917
War Diary	(G.34.c.7.4.)	23/06/1917	25/06/1917
War Diary	Reninghelst. M4	26/06/1917	27/06/1917
War Diary	R.32.d.9.5.	28/06/1917	30/06/1917
War Diary	Le Roukloshille R.32.d.9.5	30/06/1917	22/07/1917
War Diary	M.17.a Central	23/07/1917	23/07/1917
War Diary	M.11.c.4.8	24/07/1917	11/08/1917
War Diary	R.19.d.5.2. Sht 27 S.E.	14/08/1917	22/08/1917
War Diary	Acquin V.16.a.5.0.	23/08/1917	31/08/1917
War Diary	Acquin V.16.a.5.0 Sheet 27A S.E.	01/09/1917	13/09/1917
War Diary	Le Nieppe	14/09/1917	14/09/1917
War Diary	Mont De Cats.	15/09/1917	16/09/1917
War Diary	N.16.a.7.6.	17/09/1917	23/09/1917
War Diary	Caistre W.2.c.2.2	24/09/1917	25/09/1917
War Diary	I.6.c.9.2. (Sht 27)	26/09/1917	26/09/1917
War Diary	J.2.a.2.2. (Sht 19)	27/09/1917	27/09/1917

War Diary	W.15.b.3.9. (Sht 11)	28/09/1917	30/09/1917
War Diary	La Panne W.15.b.3.9 Sheet 11.	01/10/1917	06/10/1917
War Diary	La Panne	07/10/1917	07/10/1917
War Diary	Zeepanne	08/10/1917	15/10/1917
War Diary	Zeepanne W.18.a.2.5. Sheet 11	16/10/1917	29/10/1917
War Diary	Coudekerque Branche H.11.c.3.5	30/10/1917	31/10/1917
War Diary	S Martino Italy	01/03/1918	04/03/1918
War Diary	Pommera Sheet France Lens II 4.F.20.15.	05/03/1918	20/03/1918
War Diary	Forceville Lens II	21/03/1918	21/03/1918
War Diary	Ribemont Amiens	22/03/1918	22/03/1918
War Diary	Achiet-Le-Petit Lens II	23/03/1918	24/03/1918
War Diary	Bucquoy	25/03/1918	25/03/1918
War Diary	St Amand	26/03/1918	26/03/1918
War Diary	Bailleulval Lens II	27/03/1918	28/03/1918
War Diary	Saulty	29/03/1918	29/03/1918
War Diary	Authie	30/03/1918	31/03/1918
War Diary	Authie Lens II	01/04/1918	01/04/1918
War Diary	Marieux	02/04/1918	02/04/1918
War Diary	Orville	03/04/1918	03/04/1918
War Diary	Map Hazebrouck 5A	04/04/1918	04/04/1918
War Diary	Sheet 27 L.3.b.5.6	05/04/1918	07/04/1918
War Diary	Sheet 28 H.16.a.6.4	08/04/1918	10/04/1918
War Diary	Sheet 28 G.4.a.3.0.	11/04/1918	26/04/1918
War Diary	Sheet 28. A.16.a.8.5.	27/04/1918	27/04/1918
War Diary	Sheet 27 F.28.c.8.4.	28/04/1918	01/05/1918
War Diary	Sheet 27 F.27.a.5.5	02/05/1918	31/05/1918
War Diary	Field Sheet 27 F.27.a.5.5	01/06/1918	03/06/1918
War Diary	Zegger Cappel	04/06/1918	04/06/1918
War Diary	Bleue Maison	05/06/1918	18/06/1918
War Diary	27A NE and 27A SE L.19.c.2.6.	19/06/1918	25/06/1918
War Diary	Sheet 27 NE J.22.d.3.4.	26/06/1918	30/06/1918
War Diary	Map Ref Sheet 27 K.26.c.4.8	01/07/1918	02/07/1918
War Diary	Map Ref Sheet 27 K.27.a.3.10	03/07/1918	17/07/1918
War Diary	K.26.d.7.9	18/07/1918	31/07/1918
War Diary	27 K.26.d.7.9.	01/08/1918	28/08/1918
War Diary	Renescure	29/08/1918	29/08/1918
War Diary	Hallines	30/08/1918	01/09/1918
War Diary	Abeele	02/09/1918	02/09/1918
War Diary	K.18.c.7.9	03/09/1918	06/09/1918
War Diary	27/L.28.b.2.4	07/09/1918	27/09/1918
War Diary	28/G.11.a.0.0	28/09/1918	01/10/1918
War Diary	28/H.36.b.8.4.	02/10/1918	04/10/1918
War Diary	28/H.24.c.3.2	05/10/1918	06/10/1918
War Diary	28/G.19.b.9.8.	07/10/1918	12/10/1918
War Diary	28/H.24.d.95.90	13/10/1918	16/10/1918
War Diary	Dadizeele Sheet 28 K.18.c.0.9	17/10/1918	19/10/1918
War Diary	29/G.20.c.2.0	20/10/1918	21/10/1918
War Diary	29/G.29.c.6.5.	21/10/1918	29/10/1918
War Diary	29/H.32.d.9.2.	30/10/1918	02/11/1918
War Diary	29/N.6.a.2.6	03/11/1918	04/11/1918
War Diary	29/I.26.d.0.0.	05/11/1918	07/11/1918
War Diary	29/I.3.b.3.6.	08/11/1918	10/11/1918
War Diary	29/J.34.0.0.	11/11/1918	13/11/1918
War Diary	30/N.17.a.1.9.	14/11/1918	18/11/1918
War Diary	30/V.24.c.3.3.	19/11/1918	20/11/1918
War Diary	30/U.2.d.4.4.	21/11/1918	30/11/1918

War Diary	Everbecq 30/U.2.d.4.4.	01/12/1918	12/12/1918
War Diary	Tembroek	13/12/1918	13/12/1918
War Diary	Saintes	14/12/1918	14/12/1918
War Diary	Wauthier Chateau	15/12/1918	16/12/1918
War Diary	Plancenoit	17/12/1918	17/12/1918
War Diary	Rigenee	18/12/1918	18/12/1918
War Diary	Sombreffe.	19/12/1918	19/12/1918
War Diary	Suhrlee	20/12/1918	20/12/1918
War Diary	Otreppe	21/12/1918	21/12/1918
War Diary	Villers Le Bouillet	22/12/1918	22/12/1918
War Diary	Huy	23/12/1918	31/12/1918
War Diary	Huy Liegey	01/01/1919	09/01/1919
War Diary	Scharrenbroich (Rosrath) Sheet 26 Germany.	10/01/1919	12/01/1919
War Diary	Scharrenbroich Rosrath Sheet 22 Germany.	13/01/1919	28/02/1919
War Diary	Scharrenbroich Rosrath	01/03/1919	10/04/1919
War Diary	Scharrenbroich	11/04/1919	25/04/1919
War Diary	Scharrenbroich Rosrath	26/04/1919	13/05/1919
War Diary	Heumar	14/05/1919	19/06/1919
War Diary	Overath	20/06/1919	30/06/1919
War Diary	Rath Heumar	01/07/1919	31/10/1919
Miscellaneous	No 2 Coy 41st Divisional Train. Appendix I	01/01/1917	01/01/1917

WO95/2631/4
297 Coy ASC

BEF
41 Div Train

297 Coy ASC

1916 MAY — 1917 OCT
1918 MAR — 1919 OCT

IN ITALY 1917 NOV — 1918 FEB

WAR DIARY
or
INTELLIGENCE SUMMARY
(Erase heading not required.)

Army Form C. 2118

Place	Date	Hour	Summary of Events and Information	Remarks and references to Appendices
NOOTE BOOM F.m.C.b.5 Sheet 36A	8/5/16		Supplying following units 12th East Surreys, 15th Hants, 11th R.W. Kents, 18th K.R.R. 228 Coy R.E. 122 Byde H.Q. and their Coy. T/Lieut R.N. Galbraith took command of this Coy vice T/Capt. R.N. Kemp.	
do	9/5/16		Supplies as above. Orders from B.H.Q. to move to A.6.d.8.6. (Sheet 36) at 12.30 tomorrow, 10th inst.	
	10/5/16		Sunds, 1 Rider (No 4) and 1 H.D. (No 41) to M.V.S. Marched at 12.30 via NOOTE BOOM and STEENWERCK to LA CRECHE (A6 d.8.6.) ascertained that no claim would be made for damages by owner of either of two farms vacated.	
LA CRECHE B.1.C.3.6 (Sheet 36)	11/5/16		138 Field Ambulance added to units supplied by this Coy. Visited Town H.Q. Drew 900 francs from Field Cashier at BAILLEUL.	
do	12/5/16		T/36555 Pte Ford G. transferred to No. 4 Coy. via S.A./141 Pte Picks (name panel) to this Coy.	
do	13/5/16		a/Corpl King H. took ill when proceeding to STRAZEELE and was sent to 27th Field Ambulance. H.Q. Divisional R.E. asked to units now being supplied by this Coy.	

WAR DIARY
or
INTELLIGENCE SUMMARY
(Erase heading not required.)

Army Form C. 2118

Place	Date	Hour	Summary of Events and Information	Remarks and references to Appendices
LA CRECHE	14/5/16		a/Corpl KING H. Struck off strength (to Base Hospital)	Considerable rain.
do	15/5/16		1 Rider (No.4) which was transferred to M.V.S. on 10th not having been sent on to Vet. Hospital NEUFCHATEL is struck off strength. H.Q. and A Battery of 187 Brigade returned by the Coy for this day only. Heavy trans[port] heart due N.W.R.	Weather very fair.
do	16/5/16		Colonel Notary called.	
do	17/5/16		T2/083066 Dr Russell T. transferred to No.1 Coy. Shoe fine made to this Coy. T2/SR/103744 Dr Rudge A. transferred to No.1 Coy vice T2/SR/103744 Dr Rudge A. Shoe fine made for Signals. The following units are now being returned to this Coy: 12th East Surreys 228 Co. R.E. 17th Machine 237 Co. R.E. 15th Hants B.H.Q. (Gunners) D.Batty 182 Brigade 11th R.West Kents H.Q. Div. R.E. 2 Coy A.S.C. 12th K.R.R. 138 Field Ambulance 233 Co. R.E.	Weather chill very fine.
	18/5/16		V.O. called. R.O. scanned men.	
	19/5/16		Visited Tran H.Q. & Returns as on my sick lines. Agreed to have attached No.1 Coy wagon of which horses Placed Corpl. Churchill in arrest — pending as ready.	

1875 Wt. W593/826 1,000,000 4/15 J.B.C. & A. A.D.S.S./Forms/C. 2118.

WAR DIARY or INTELLIGENCE SUMMARY

Army Form C. 2118

Place	Date	Hour	Summary of Events and Information	Remarks and references to Appendices
La Creche	20.5.16 21.5.16 22.5.16		Usual routine. 21.5.16 Report re light m A 6 d. 8. 7.	
	23.5.16		Gave coy of Rifles limber repaired. Ditto P.E. Limber. C.O.'s inspection of Units. Repaired wagon from m Rifles Limbers.	
	24.5.16		Usual routine. Repaired brake bar on 296 coy wagon.	
	25.5.16		Men examined by Lt. Elliott & 18 R.F.A. — no cases of Itch. Sir Mays Ghub & found in Col. F. wagon. Actions ordain for Rw. Kent.	
	26.5.16		Received various instructions re transport supply for units moving up. Paid men. No. 1 Coy came to La Creche.	
	27.5.16		Transport Accounts taking — over to Capt Kemp. The adjt 3 am. C.O. & adjt called. Reported to B.H.Q. The	
	28.5.16		Horses attacked from No 3 Cy. 2nd Y/ones. (Rest 36). Drawing Rights in A.6.d.8.7. (Rest 36).	
	29.5.16		Called at H.H.Q. re above. Went Thro' argument busy with Capt Kemp. Capt Robinson had interview with Genl Lawford. Inspection re C.R.M. Plan	
	30.5.16		Viewed newly engaged new billets in La Creche Village — instructions to move tomorrow.	
	31.5.16		Coy moved to A 5 d 5.9 Sheet 36.	

WAR DIARY
or
INTELLIGENCE SUMMARY
(Erase heading not required.)

Army Form C. 2118

Place	Date	Hour	Summary of Events and Information	Remarks and references to Appendices
LA CRECHE A 5.d.5.9 (Sheet 36)	1.6.16		Rearrangement of Brigade Groups. Usual Routine. Visited first line transport of four Battalions.	A.T.G.
"	2.6.16		Usual Routine. G.O.C. visited Camp.	A.T.G.
"	3.6.16		Do. Saw first line transport of 138th FIELD AMBULANCE. Three drivers returned by 138th FIELD AMBULANCE and 3 others sent to that unit.	A.T.G.
"	4.6.16		Usual Routine. Visited all four Battalions re first line transport.	A.T.G.
"	5.6.16		Do. T/35672 Driver Wn E.A. transferred to H.Q. Coy vice T4/058084 Dr. Sparrow A.J.R. transferred to this Coy.	A.T.G.
"	6.6.16		Usual Routine. T4/057437 a/Sergt. CHURCHILL W.A.M. transferred to H.Q. Coy vice T3/027039 a/Sergt. ROBERTSON transferred to this Coy.	A.T.G.
"	7.6.16		Usual Routine.	A.T.G.
"	8.6.16		T/36777 Dr. HARRIS F.A. evacuated to BASE HOSPITAL. Struck off strength.	A.T.G.

WAR DIARY or INTELLIGENCE SUMMARY

Army Form C. 2118

(Erase heading not required.)

Place	Date	Hour	Summary of Events and Information	Remarks and references to Appendices
LA CRECHE	9.6.16		Usual Routine. T3/027805 Pte PARKER W. from 1st Gen. H.T. Depot taken on Strength.	SAA
"	10.6.16		Do. Very heavy rain.	SAA
"	11.6.16		Do.	SAA
"	12.6.16		Do.	SAA
"	13.6.16		Vickers Brigade - first line transport.	SAA
"	14.6.16		T5/8966 Saddr. Dr. BRADY M, T4/094275 Dr MILBURN J and T/35519 Dr PERKINS R.W. evacuated to No. 8 Casualty Clearing Station & struck off Strength.	SAA
"	15.6.16		Do. T2/026772 Dr McPHAIL L evacuated to Base and struck off.	SAA
"	16.6.16		Do. Gas Alarm 12.30 am	SAA
"	17.6.16		Do.	SAA
"	18.6.16		Do.	SAA
"	19.6.16		Vickers Brigade - first line transport.	SAA
"	20.6.16		Inspection by C.O. Gas Alarm 12.15 am	SAA
"	21.6.16 22.6.16 23.6.16		Do.	SAA

WAR DIARY or INTELLIGENCE SUMMARY

Army Form C. 2118

Place	Date	Hour	Summary of Events and Information	Remarks and references to Appendices
LA CRÈCHE	24.6.16		Usual Routine. T/S/Sadd. & BRADY M. and T/22536 & CHIDGAY H transferred from Reinforcement station and taken on strength.	A.D.S.
	25.6.16		Usual Routine. T/094275 & MILBURN D reported from No 8 casualty clearing station taken on strength.	A.D.S.
	26.6.16		do.	A.D.S.
	27.6.16		do. Visited 138 Field Ambulance.	
	28.6.16		do.	A.D.S.
	29.6.16		Double Refill in place of usual routine. Inspected first line transport	A.D.S.
	30.6.16		Tonks returns to Supply Column at FLÈTRE instead of refilling point.	A.D.S.

No 2 Coy. 41st Divisional Train.

WAR DIARY or **INTELLIGENCE SUMMARY**

Army Form C. 2118

Place	Date	Hour	Summary of Events and Information	Remarks and references to Appendices
LA CRECHE A5.d.5.9. Sheet 36	1.7.16		Usual Routine: Reveille 4 a.m. Stables 4.30 a.m., 11.30 a.m. and 5.30 p.m. Meals, 5.30 a.m. 12.30 p.m. and 5.30 p.m. Railhead 7 a.m. Refilling 8 a.m. Lights Out 9 p.m. A.D.V.S. inspected	ADS
	2.7.16		Usual Routine	ADS
	3.7.16		Do. Visited First Line Transport	ADS
	4.7.16		Do. G.O.C. visited Camp.	ADS
	5.7.16		Do. Accoustic Convoy 10 p.m.	ADS
	6.7.16		Do.	ADS
	7.7.16		Do. Attended Court Martial on T3/023745 Dr YOXALL A at LE BIZET. Capt E.B. ROBINSON A.S.C. (Supply Officer) admitted to 138 FIELD AMBULANCE. Lieut H MORRIS A.S.C. posted to the Coy. as S.O.	ADS
	8.7.16		Do. Visited First Line Transport. T/35519 Dr PERKINS R.W. Returned from No 4 Staty Hosp! 6th inst and taken on Strength.	ADS
	9.7.16		Do. Horse inspection by C.O.	ADS
	10.7.16		Do. 1 H.D. horse (No. 23) sent to 73rd Coy Mobile Vety. Hosp!.	ADS
	11.7.16		Railhead 6 a.m. Refill 10 a.m.	ADS
	12.7.16		Resumed usual routine.	ADS
	13.7.16		Usual Routine. Visited First Line Transport	ADS

Army Form C. 2118

WAR DIARY
or
INTELLIGENCE SUMMARY
(Erase heading not required.)

No 7 Coy. A/of Divisional Train

Place	Date	Hour	Summary of Events and Information	Remarks and references to Appendices
LA CRECHE A 5 d 59 Sheet 36.	14.7.16		Usual Routine.	
	15.7.16		do	
	16.7.16		do 1 H.D. horse No. 51 sent to 52nd M.V. Sect.	
	17.7.16		do Above horse evacuated to BASE and struck off strength. H.D. horse No 23 returned from 73rd Coy. M.V. Hosp.l. Visited first line transport.	
	18.7.16		do T/13938 Dr BANNER N admitted to 138th Field Ambulance.	
	19.7.16		do Capt E.S. ROBINSON A.S.C. evacuated to BASE and subsequently invalided to England 6.7.16 struck off strength. Lieut W. SEGRAVE proceeded to BETHUNE to join Royal Flying Corps. Accessories convoy 4.30 p.m.	
	20.7.16		do T/13938 Dr BANNER.N. discharged from 138th F.Ambulance. Lieut W.H. SEGRAVE struck off strength.	
	21.7.16		do T3/026231 Dr McNEE D admitted to 138 Field Ambulance. Received warning to be ready to move at short notice.	
	22.7.16		do	
	23.7.16		do	
	24.7.16		do Accessories convoy 11.15 p.m. from actg Adjutant.	
	25.7.16		do T3/026231 Dr McNEE D discharged No.50 C.C.S. T4/108222 Dr HATCH J.W. admitted 138 Field Ambulance	DAG

… **Army Form C. 2118**

No 2 Coy. 41st Divisional Train

WAR DIARY
or
INTELLIGENCE SUMMARY
(Erase heading not required.)

Instructions regarding War Diaries and Intelligence Summaries are contained in F.S. Regs., Part II. and the Staff Manual respectively. Title Pages will be prepared in manuscript.

Place	Date	Hour	Summary of Events and Information	Remarks and references to Appendices
La CRÈCHE A 5.d.5.9 Sheet 36.	26/7/16		Usual Routine. Heavy firing 11 p.m.	
	27/7/16		Do Marching order parade (dismounted) by C.O.	
	28/7/16		Do	
	29/7/16		Do 1st Brigade moved to Divisional Reserve — changed Battalion billets.	
	30/7/16		Do	
	31/7/16		Do Lieut Tripp A.S.C. joined Coy. Commenced watering at S29 B 6 8. Sheet 28.	D.T.G.

D. T. Galbraith Capt
Comdg No 2 Coy
41st Divisional Train
A.S.C.

No. 2 Coy. 41st Divisional Train A.S.C.

WAR DIARY
or
INTELLIGENCE SUMMARY

Army Form C. 2118

Place	Date	Hour	Summary of Events and Information	Remarks and references to Appendices
LA CRÈCHE A5d.5.9. Sheet 36.	1.8.16		Usual Routine: Reveille 4 am. Stables 4.30 am. 11.30 am. and 3.30 pm. Extra evening feed 8 pm. Meals 5.30 am. 12.30 pm. and 5.30 pm. Railhead 7 am. Repelling 8 am. Lights out 9 pm. Rationing the following units:- 21st Antiaircraft Battery. 9th Kite Balloon Section 41st Trench Mortar Bty. 41st Trench Warfare School 122 Machine Gun Coy. 138 Field Ambulance 226 Coy. R.E. 145 Army Troops Coy R.E. Cavalry Details (570) 119 Siege Battery R.G.A. 150th Heavy Battery R.G.A. H.Q. 187 Bde R.F.A. A.B.C. and D Batteries of 187 Brigade R.F.A. 122 Brigade H.Q. 12th East Surreys. 15th Hants. 11th West Kents. 18th K.R.R. No. Coy 41st D.T. Total 6705 men. 321 H.D. horses 894 L.D. horses 133 mules. General LAWFORD visited the Camp. Very hot. Paid men.	
	2.8.16		Usual Routine. Visited First Line Transport.	Very hot
	3.8.16		Do. T4/108222 Dr HATCH J.W. evacuated to No. 15 Casualty Clearing Station and struck off strength. Conference re reduction or increase of Motorisation Equipment.	Very hot. A.T.G.

WAR DIARY or INTELLIGENCE SUMMARY

Army Form C. 2118

Instructions regarding War Diaries and Intelligence Summaries are contained in F.S. Regs., Part II. and the Staff Manual respectively. Title Pages will be prepared in manuscript.

(Erase heading not required.)

Place	Date	Hour	Summary of Events and Information	Remarks and references to Appendices
LA CRECHE A5d.5.9. Sheet 36	4.8.16		Usual Routine.	
	5.8.16		Do. Water to be drawn from tanks at A.4.c.8.6. (Sheet 36) from this date. On reorganization of H.T. of Train 9 H.D. horses were this day sent to a New Zealand Division. Two H.D. were received by this Coy from No.1 Coy and 6 Mules were received from the NEW ZEALAND Division. Gas alert 8 p.m.	
	6.8.16		Usual Routine. Weather: very warm	
	7.8.16		Do. Do	
	8.8.16		Do. G.O.C. commented on excellence of turnout at Railhead Do	
	9.8.16		Do. H.D. 87 sent to Mobile Vet'y Hospital. (not struck off) Inspected Ft. Transport Do	
	10.8.16		Do. Do slight rain	
	11.8.16		Do. Weather: warm	
	12.8.16		Do. " Sultry.	
	13.8.16		Do. Reception by G.O.C. at D.H.Q. " "	
	14.8.16		Do. THE KING passed through A.12.a. (Sheet 36) Instructions received for forthcoming move. slight rain.	
CAESTRE W.2.b.9.8 Sheet 27	15.8.16		Do. up to delivery of rations to units. Company paraded at 1.30 p.m. and proceeded by Route March to CAESTRE W.2.b.9.8 Sheet 27 via NOOTE BOOM OULTERSTEENE and STRAZEELE arriving at 5.50 p.m. Approximate distance 12 miles. Accommodation for men, one barn holding 40 men. officers billeted. Horses on lines – earth standing. No casualties on march. some Rain.	W.G.

WAR DIARY
or
INTELLIGENCE SUMMARY

(Erase heading not required.)

Army Form C. 2118

Place	Date	Hour	Summary of Events and Information	Remarks and references to Appendices
CAESTRE W2f9c Sheet 27	16.8.16		Reveille 5:30. Railed at CAESTRE Railway Station 12 noon. Refill on camp ground at 2pm. Average distance of units 2½ miles.	Weather Cool.
	17.8.16		Reveille 5am. Railhead for bread and meat 6:30am; for groceries 8am. Refill 1 pm. C.O. orders Camp.	Warm: Some rain. Cool.
	18.8.16		Reveille 5am. Railhead 6:15 and 8 am. Refill 9am.	Cool.
	19.8.16		Routine as above.	Fine.
	20.8.16		Received instructions re move.	No
	21.8.16		Lt C TRIPP ASC. proceeded by train to new area for billeting purposes. Drew 114 remounts from railhead for distribution to units of Division. One H.D. horse received from Remounts taken on strength.	Fine
	22.8.16		Railed 8:30 and 10 am. Refill 11 am (delayed) Section on 9th inst struck off strength. One H.D. horse sent to MOBILE VET. Double issue to 2 units	
	23.8.16		Railed 9 and 10 am. Refill following. Double issue to remaining units.	
	24.8.16		No railhead or refill. Proceeded at 8.50 am by route march to BAILLEUL (MAIN STATION) via FLETRE and METEREN, arriving there at 11 am. Entrainment of horses and vehicles took 35 minutes. Train left at 2:30; via CALAIS BOULOGNE and ABBEVILLE to LONGPRES-LES-CORPS-SAINTS; arrived midnight. Detrainment completed at 2 am. Marched to new camp at Long. *(continued next page)*	
LONG Square ① ⑥ Map 1/100000 ABBEVILLE 14.	25.8.16			

Army Form C. 2118

WAR DIARY
or
INTELLIGENCE SUMMARY
(Erase heading not required.)

Instructions regarding War Diaries and Intelligence Summaries are contained in F.S. Regs., Part II. and the Staff Manual respectively. Title Pages will be prepared in manuscript.

Place	Date	Hour	Summary of Events and Information	Remarks and references to Appendices
LONG (Howard Map) (ABBEVILLE 1A Square L 6)	25.8.16		Arrived 3 am. Men bivouacked. Reveille 6.30. Rations dumped by Supply Column on MOUFLERS - AILLY LE HAUT CLOCHER Rd on mile N.W. of MOUFLERS. Refill 10 am.	Slight rain
	26.8.16		Reveille 5 am. Refill 9 am. Remaining routine as usual. TS/8393 Dr. S.Sm. TASKER.W. brought from 138 FIELD AMBULANCE and replaced by TS/7287 Dr. S.Sm. TWEED. R.F.A.	Warm
	27.8.16		Routine as above. T/28156 Dr. GEORGE A.E. admitted 138 FIELD AMBULANCE	Heavy rain
	28.8.16		do G.O.C. visited lines.	do.
	29.8.16		do except refill which was 10.30 (in error).	do
	30.8.16		do Camp partly flooded. Billets found for part of men.	do
	31.8.16		do	Fine

W. G. [signature] Capt
Comdg.

No. 2 COMPANY,
41st
DIVISIONAL TRAIN.
No. ....
Date 31.8.16

W.S.G.

1875 Wt. W593/826 1,000,000 4/15 J.B.C. & A. A.D.S.S./Forms/C.2118.

No 2 Coy 41st Divisional Train
ASC

WAR DIARY
or
INTELLIGENCE SUMMARY
(Erase heading not required.)

Army Form C. 2118

Instructions regarding War Diaries and Intelligence Summaries are contained in F. S. Regs., Part II. and the Staff Manual respectively. Title Pages will be prepared in manuscript.

Place	Date	Hour	Summary of Events and Information	Weather	Remarks and references to Appendices
LONG. Map ABBEVILLE No. 14. 1/100,000 Square (L) (6).	1.9.16	Routine.	Reveille 5am. Stables 5:30 to 6:30 am., 11:30 to 12:30 noon, 4 to 5:15 pm. Meals 6:30 a.m. 12:30 noon 5:30 pm. Refill on MOUFLERS - AILLY Road at 9 a.m.	Fine	
	2.9.16	Routine as above		Fine	
	3.9.16	Ditto.	Divisional Horse Show and Sports. Coy. took 1st Prize for best turnout of 2 H.D. horses in Divisional wagon and there 1st Prize for best turned out pair of Mules. H.D. horse No. 80 and to 52nd MOBILE VETERINARY SECTION and struck off strength.	Some rain.	
	4.9.16	Routine as above except that there were two Refills. T/28156 Dr. GEORGE A.E. discharged from 140th FIELD AMBULANCE		Cloudy	
	5.9.16	Company wagons and Supply wagons proceeded by Divisional Route March to ARGŒUVES (16 miles) via FLIXECOURT and BELLOY-SUR-SOMME (where we watered) Arrived ARGŒUVES 6 p.m. One riding horse (grey gelding No 77) went lame and was left at BELLOY-SUR-SOMME; struck off strength from this date in Train Order No. Supply wagons sent to units.	Rain	
ARGŒUVES Map AMIENS 17 M/100,000 Square © ①	6.9.16	Company wagons proceeded by Route March to BUIRE-SUR-L'ANCRE via AMIENS and QUERRIEU (2½ hrs halt) Distance 23 miles Started 6:45 am. Arrived 6:30 p.m. a/FARR. CORPL. TODD.W. proceeded to 138 FIELD AMBULANCE. Refilled on arrival	Fine T5/6483	
BUIRE-SUR-L'ANCRE D24.C.0.8 Sheet 62D.	7.9.16	Refilled at 9 a.m. and 4 p.m. on road 1 mile N. of BUIRE.	Fine	

No. 2 Coy 41st Divisional Train
ABC

WAR DIARY
or
INTELLIGENCE SUMMARY

Army Form C. 2118

Place	Date	Hour	Summary of Events and Information	Weather	Remarks and references to Appendices
BUIRE-SUR-L'ANCRE Sheet 62D D.24.d.9.0.	8.9.16		Usual Routine in Camp. Refilled at 1.30 p.m. Reveille Baggage wagons	Fine	
	9.9.16		Do.	Do.	
	10.9.16		Do. No refile.	Do.	
ALBERT Sheet 62D E.10.b.1.5	11.9.16		Company wagons proceeded at 10 am. by Route March to new camp South of ALBERT on the ALBERT-MEAULTE Road (Sheet 62D E.10.b.1.5) Distance 3½ miles Arrived 11.50 a.m. Supply wagons refilled at BUIRE at 1.30 p.m. and proceeded to units camped at F.8.c (Sheet 62D)	Some rain.	
	12.9.16		Routine:- Reveille 5.45 a.m. Stables 6-7, 11-12, 4-5.15 Meals 7am. 12.30, 5.30. All wagons (including Supply Section) called in and used for general fatigues of 41st Division. Units drew supplies from Refilling Point at FRICOURT F.3.c.1.0 (Sheet 62D) on their own first line transport Refilling hour 11.45 am. H.D. horse No 22 sent to 52nd MOBILE VETY SECN and struck off strength	Some rain.	
	13.9.16		Camp routine as yesterday. Refilling as yesterday. Supply train 4 hours late.	Rain in evening	
	14.9.16		Do. but drew supplies for units in supply wagons. Baggage wagons sent to units. Warned re a move.	Fine	

No 2 Coy 41st Divnl Train
ABC

Army Form C. 2118

WAR DIARY
or
INTELLIGENCE SUMMARY
(Erase heading not required.)

Instructions regarding War Diaries and Intelligence Summaries are contained in F.S. Regs., Part II. and the Staff Manual respectively. Title Pages will be prepared in manuscript.

Place	Date	Hour	Summary of Events and Information	Remarks and references to Appendices
ALBERT Sheet 62 D E.10.b.1.5.	15.9.16		Same routine in camp but standing to from 9am in anticipation of move to new camp at F.5.d.4.8 (Sheet 62 D) Supplies drawn in Supply wagons as yesterday. 41st Division advanced on LES BOEUFS – FLERS line : 122 Brigade on FLERS.	fine
	16.9.16		Usual routine in camp : still on short notice to move. Supplies delivered in Company Supply wagons as yesterday. Adjoining camp shelled at 6 p.m.	do
	17.9.16		Reveillé sharred to MONTAUBAN Refill not completed till 5.30 p.m. to MAMETZ cancelled. Supply wagons move with units in view of move.	do
	18.9.16		Left camp with Company wagons only & proceeded (at 9.15 am) by route march to old camp at BUIRE-SUR-L'ANCRE. Arrived 10.10 am. ALBERT – VIVIER MILL Road at 11 am. Baggage & supply wagons Refilled on route brought in. Baggage & supply wagons	heavy rain
BUIRE-SUR-L'ANCRE	19.9.16		Routine : Stables 6–7, 11–12, 4–5.15 Meals following stables. Refilled on BUIRE – DERNANCOURT Road at 11 am. DR DODSON.W. and T4/057521 DR WOTHERSPOON. D admitted to 140th FIELD AMBULANCE T/36754	slight rain
	20.9.16		Usual Routine in Camp. Refilled 9am. Baggage section took supplies to H.Q. Coy. the H.D. horse sent to M.V. HOSPITAL (attached horse from H.Q. Coy) Inspection by A.D.V.S.	do

No 2 Coy 42nd Divisional Train
ASC

WAR DIARY
or
INTELLIGENCE SUMMARY

Army Form C. 2118

Place	Date	Hour	Summary of Events and Information	Weather	Remarks and references to Appendices
BUIRE-SUR L'ANCRE D24.c.0.8. Map 62.D.	21.9.16		Usual Camp Routine. Refill 9 a.m. Lieut. H.V. CUSACK of this Coy. temporarily attached to No.1 Coy.	Cold and Damp	
	22.9.16		ditto. ditto. Sent 5 pair for conveyance of Divisional Troops supplies. H.D. horse No 83 died (enteritis) Baggage wagons sent to units returned to duty T/36754 Dr DODSON. W. and T4/057521 Dr WOTHERSPOON D.	do	
	23.9.16		Usual Routine. H.D. horse No 63 struck off strength. T.S./8483 a/FARR.CORPL. TODD. W. who proceeded to 138 HELD AMBULANCE # is struck off strength from that date and reverts to permanent grade of Shoeing-Smith on transfer.	fine	
	24.9.16		Routine as above. Two H.D horses and one rider received from REMOUNTS Yesterday are taken on strength.	fine	
	25.9.16		Routine as above. Reported on First Line Transport of 122 BRIGADE.	fine	
	26.9.16		Usual Routine.	fine	
	27.9.16		ditto	Heavy Rain	
	28.9.16		ditto	Rain	

No 2 Coy 41st Divisional Train A.S.C.

WAR DIARY or **INTELLIGENCE SUMMARY**

Army Form C. 2118

Place	Date	Hour	Summary of Events and Information	Remarks and references to Appendices
BUIRE SUR L'ANCRE	29.9.16		Usual Routine. T4/057504 Dr Arnold A. admitted to 138th Field Ambulance.	Fine rain.
D.24.c.0.8 Sheet 62D	30.9.16		Usual Routine	Fine

D.R. Galbraith Capt
O.C. No 2 Coy
41st Divisional Train
A.S.C.

Army Form C. 2118

WAR DIARY
or
INTELLIGENCE SUMMARY
(Erase heading not required.)

No 2 Coy. 41 st Divisional Train. A.S.C.

Instructions regarding War Diaries and Intelligence Summaries are contained in F.S. Regs., Part II. and the Staff Manual respectively. Title Pages will be prepared in manuscript.

Place	Date	Hour	Summary of Events and Information	Remarks and references to Appendices
BUIRE S/L'ANCRE D.24. c.0.8 Sheet 62 D	1.10.16		Usual Routine, viz:- Reveille 5.45 a.m. Stables 6-7, 11-12, 4-5.15. Meals following Stables. Refill 9 a.m. Men bathed at VIVIER MILL	Weather. Slight Rain.
	2.10.16		Proceeded by Route March to BÉCORDEL - BÉCOURT, (F7.C.5.7. Sheet 62 D) Started 10.15 a.m. Arrived 1 p.m. Distance by fine weather track 4½ miles. Refilled at BUIRE at 8.30 a.m. and Supply wagons marched with the Company; no guides having arrived they were despatched to units at 3 p.m. and returned at midnight. T4/057504 Dvr ARNOLD. A. discharged from 138 Field Ambulance	Heavy Rain.
BÉCORDEL - BÉCOURT F.7.C.5.7 Sheet 62 D.	3.10.16		Usual Routine. Refill 10 a.m. Baggage Wagons not returned (by order of BRIGADIER-GENERAL TOWSEY.) T4/065304	Rain
	4.10.16		Usual Routine. Refill 1 p.m. (Lorries late.) T4/065301 Dvr GIBBONS. F. transferred to 138th FIELD AMBULANCE on 3rd inst and struck off strength from this date. T3/023745 Dvr YOXALL. A. returned to duty.	Rain.
	5.10.16		Usual Routine. Refill 9.30 a.m. Baggage wagons returned.	Slight Showers
	6.10.16		Do. LIEUT H.V. CUSACK proceeded to M.T. SCHOOL OF INSTRUCTION for a Short Course.	Cold and damp

No 2 Coy AHS Divisional Train ASC

WAR DIARY
or
INTELLIGENCE SUMMARY
(Erase heading not required.)

Army Form C. 2118

Instructions regarding War Diaries and Intelligence Summaries are contained in F. S. Regs., Part II. and the Staff Manual respectively. Title Pages will be prepared in manuscript.

Place	Date	Hour	Summary of Events and Information	Remarks and references to Appendices
BÉCORDEL -BÉCOURT F.7.C.5.7 Sheet 62.D.	8.10.16		Usual Routine in Camp. Drew Rations in bulk at ALBERT Station (Railhead) at 11 am (Standing by from 6 am) Refilled at BÉCORDEL at 1.30 pm. T4/110341 Dr FINCH. O. Struck by Shell splinter at ALBERT.	Cold & damp.
	9.10.16		Usual Routine in Camp. Railhead 11.30 am. Refill 1.30 pm	Showery
	10.10.16		do " 3 pm " 4.30 " MAMETZ Road clothes and supplies not delivered till 10.30 pm	dull
	11.10.16		Company moved to DERNANCOURT (E.15.a.3.5 Sheet 62.D) Railhead ALBERT Refill 1 pm.	still
DERNANCOURT E.15.a.3.5 Sheet 62.D.	12.10.16		Usual Company Routine. Railhead 10.30 am. (Standing by from 7 am) Refill 11.30 am	do.
	13.10.16		Usual Routine Railhead 8.30 am. Refill 9.30 am. Lieut C.TRIPP detached for duty with No.1 Coy. S2/616374 Pte BATCHELOR G and T4/092223 Dr TURNER W admitted to 139 R FIELD AMBULANCE	do.
	14.10.16		Usual Routine Railhead EDGE HILL 4 pm. (Standing by from 9 am.) Refill 5 pm	Fine
	15.10.16		do do 4 pm Refill 5 pm	dull.

Army Form C. 2118

WAR DIARY
or
INTELLIGENCE SUMMARY
(Erase heading not required.)

No. 61 4th Divisional Train A.S.C.

Instructions regarding War Diaries and Intelligence Summaries are contained in F.S. Regs., Part II. and the Staff Manual respectively. Title Pages will be prepared in manuscript.

Place	Date	Hour	Summary of Events and Information	Remarks and references to Appendices
DERNANCOURT	16.10.16		Proceeded at 8.50.a.m. by Route March to ARGOEUVES arriving at 6.15.pm. Watered at QUERRIEU. Distance 25 miles.	Dull
ARGOEUVES Map AMIENS 17 Square 6.D.	17.10.16		Refilled at 6 am. Proceeded at 10.30 am. to HUCHENNEVILLE via PICQUIGNY HANGEST and BRAY arriving at 8.50 pm. Distance 23 miles. Very slow march.	Rain
HUCHENNEVILLE Map ABBEVILLE 7/10 Square	18.10.16		Refilled 7.30 am (two days supplies) Second Refill 11 pm ("hard tack" for train journey on 20th): this was delivered in baggage waggons. S2/016237 Pte BATCHELOR.G. discharged from XIV Corps REST STATION on 18th reported for duty.	Heavy Rain.
	19.10.16		Refilled 1am. (rations for 19th) Second Refill 2.30 pm (rations for 21st to travel in Supply waggons with units)	Showery
	20.10.16		Marched at 9.30 am. to PONT REMY Railway Station and Train entrained at 1.30pm. Completed at 3 pm. Left PONT REMY 5 pm. T5/4105 Dr.S.Sm. COOK.T.H. T4/185328 Dr JONES S.C. joined from Base Depot.(H.T.+S)	Fine.
	21.10.16		Arrived at GODEWAERSVELDE at 4.30 am. Detrained and marched to CAESTRE arriving at 7 am. Refilled at 2 pm. on CAESTRE - EECKE Road.	Dull
CAESTRE W.2.b.9.8. Sheet 27.	22.10.16		Usual company routine. Refilled 9 am. HD Horse No.47 sent to 23rd MOBILE VETERINARY SECTION on 15th inst struck off strength this day.	Showery.
	23.10.16		Usual Routine. Refilled 9 am	Showery

1875 Wt. W593/826 1,000,000 4/15. J.B.C.&A. A.D.S.S./Forms/C. 2118.

No 2 Coy. H 1st Divisional Train A.S.C.

WAR DIARY
or
INTELLIGENCE SUMMARY
(Erase heading not required.)

Army Form C. 2118

Instructions regarding War Diaries and Intelligence Summaries are contained in F.S. Regs., Part II. and the Staff Manual respectively. Title Pages will be prepared in manuscript.

Place	Date	Hour	Summary of Events and Information	Remarks and references to Appendices
CAESTRE W2.b.9.8 Sheet 27	23-10-16		Usual Routine. Refilled 9am. Dr TURNER W (T/4/097273) evacuated to 139 R FIELD AMBULANCE on 13R inst (q.v.) Struck off strength this day.	Showery
	24-10-16		Usual Routine. 2/Lt. C.M.C. LUFF A.S.C. joined from 10R AUXILIARY (HORSE) COY. (224 COY, A.S.C.) Taken on strength R.	Do
	25-10-16		Proceeded by Route March at 8.40am to RENINGHELST arriving at 12.10 pm. Thence to be stationed. Supplies drawn from WIPPENHOEK Siding at 7.30 am. Refilled at 1pm.	Do
	26.10.16		Usual Company Routine. Railhead WIPPENHOEK 8.15am. Refilled 11 am. CAPTAIN D.D. GALBRAITH A.S.C., O.C. this Coy., proceeded on ten days leave of absence at 6pm this day.	Do
	27.10.16		Usual Routine. Railhead WIPPENHOEK 8.15 am. Refilled 11am. Four wagons proceeded to RE Workshops OUDERDOM to draw timber for Dump and Camp. D/Sdn: Cpl TOBSON T.E., 4/ Dr MURRAY M., and Dr BRADY M. were trians Cpl G.F.S.C.M.	Showery

Army Form C. 2118

No 2 Coy 41st Divisional Train A.S.C.

WAR DIARY
or
INTELLIGENCE SUMMARY
(Erase heading not required.)

Instructions regarding War Diaries and Intelligence Summaries are contained in F.S. Regs., Part II. and the Staff Manual respectively. Title Pages will be prepared in manuscript.

Place	Date	Hour	Summary of Events and Information	Remarks and references to Appendices
RENINGHELST	28/10/16	Normal Coy routine	Railed WIPPENHOEK 8.15 am. Refilled 11 am. Inspection of Camp and Stables by O.C Train. Four G.S wagons under an NCO proceeded to YPRES to convey mobile o/Sergt HASTINGS T/11241 reverted to permanent Rank of Corporal Dr GEORGE No T/8158 proceeded to 138th Field Ambulance for duty Dr HUNTER No T/027102 rejoined No 2 Coy A.S.C from 138th F. Ambulance	Showery
RENINGHELST	29/10/16	Normal Coy routine	Railed WIPPENHOER 8.15 am. Refilled 11 am. Four G.S. Wagons reported for duty with 228th Field Coy R.E. Two H.D Horses taken on strength of the Coy from Remounts.	Showery
RENINGHELST	30/10/16	Normal Coy routine	Railed WIPPENHOEK 8.15 am. Refilled 11 am. Inspection of rifles and Gas helmets by O.C of Company. Dr. FISHER 9. STA/141 and Dr EVANS.O. T/066299 proceeded to 138th FIELD AMBULANCE for duty, and were Struck off the Strength of the Company	Showery
RENINGHELST	31/10/16	Normal Coy routine	Railed WIPPENHOEK 8.15 am. Refilled 11 am. Two wagons under NCO proceeded to OUDERDOM to draw materials from RE workshops for camp use	Showery A.W.Thomas 2/Lieut A.S.C. for Major OC 41st Divl ASC

No. 2 Coy. 41st DIVISIONAL TRAIN

WAR DIARY or INTELLIGENCE SUMMARY

Army Form C. 2118

Place	Date	Hour	Summary of Events and Information	Weather	Remarks and references to Appendices
RENINGHELST M.5.c.3.8. Sheet 28	1.11.16		Usual Company Routine viz:- Reveille 4.45 a.m. Stables 5-6, 11-12, 4-5.15. Meals after stables. Lights out 9 p.m. Railhead WIPPENHOEK SIDING. (L 28 d 3.8 Sheet 27) 8.15 a.m. Rifle Butt of KASTEEL MOLEN (M.5.a.2.7. Sheet 28) 11 a.m. Rider No 78 Sent to 52nd MOBILE VETERINARY SECTION. T4/110341 Dr FINCH. O. admitted to 140th FIELD AMBULANCE.	Showery.	
	2.11.16		Routine as above. T4/108247 Dr BURGESS J. proceeded on leave to U.K.	Rain.	
	3.11.16		Do. Court Martial parade in Camp (2 and 3 Coys.)	Rain.	
	4.11.16		Do. One Limber G.S. with driver attacked for duty to 41st DIVISIONAL TRENCH WARFARE SCHOOL. T3/027003 Dr MURRAY. M. admitted to Detention Camp there to undergo 3 months F.P. No1. R.E. officer (of 228 FIELD COY. R.E.) visited camp to estimate for hutting etc required.	Rain with gale at night.	W.S.G.

Army Form C. 2118

WAR DIARY
or
INTELLIGENCE SUMMARY
(Erase heading not required.)

No 2 Coy. 41st Divisional Train.

Instructions regarding War Diaries and Intelligence Summaries are contained in F.S. Regs., Part II. and the Staff Manual respectively. Title Pages will be prepared in manuscript.

Place	Date	Hour	Summary of Events and Information	Weather	Remarks and references to Appendices
RENINGHELST M.5.c.3.8. Sheet 28.	5·11·16		Usual Company Routine. Inspection of Camp by O.C. Train	Rain and gale.	
	6·11·16		Do. Inspection of Camp by D.M.S. Ground unsatisfactory. Lack of drainage. Need of attention by R.E. LIEUT. O.W.M. SHELTON A.S.C. proceeded on leave to England	Rain	
	7·11·16		Usual Routine.	Heavy Rain	
	8·11·16		Do.	Do.	
	9·11·16		Do. Dr. FINCH. D. (evacuated to C.C.S 1/11/16) struck off strength.	Fine	
	10·11·16		Do. 1 H.D. horse received from 138th FIELD AMBULANCE.	Fine	
	11·11·16		Do.	Do.	
	12·11·16		Do. Inspection of Coy. transport by O.C. TRAIN. Coy's Box Respirators tested.	Do.	
	13·11·16		Do.	Do.	
	14·11·16		Do.	Do.	A.T.G.

No 2 Coy. 41st Divisional Train A.S.C.

WAR DIARY

~~INTELLIGENCE SUMMARY~~

(Erase heading not required.)

Army Form C. 2118

Instructions regarding War Diaries and Intelligence Summaries are contained in F.S. Regs., Part II. and the Staff Manual respectively. Title Pages will be prepared in manuscript.

Place	Date	Hour	Summary of Events and Information	Remarks and references to Appendices
RENINGHELST M5.c.3.8 Sheet 28.	15.11.16		Usual Company Routine. Lieut. C. TRIPP A.S.C., T/35647 Dr. BRAID A. and one Rider returned from duty with H.Q. Coy. T/13119 S/SSM EYCOTT. F. and T4/057256 Dr WALSHAW A. proceeded on leave to England.	Fine.
	16.11.16		Usual Routine. T2/SR.02453 Dr KEEPING. H. attached for duty with TRENCH WARFARE SCHOOL. G.O.C. visited Camp. Lieut. C. TRIPP A.S.C. proceeded on leave to England.	Fine.
	17.11.16		Usual Routine.	Do
	18.11.16		Do. Inspection of First Line Transport 122 Brigade by O.C. Train	Slight Rain
	19.11.16		Do. T4/044017 Dr. ATHERTON. F. and T/35668 Dr GOAD. T. proceeded to 138 IR FIELD AMBULANCE for duty.	Wet
	20.11.16		Do. LIEUT. H.M. MORRIS Supply Officer of this Coy. promoted Captain as from 17.9.16 subject to publication in London Gazette.	Wet
	21.11.16		Supplies drawn in bulk from train at WIPPENHOEK SIDING and refilling done alongside train. Supplies sent therefrom to units in Supply Vehicles. Reveille to Supply Section 3.30 am Refilling 7 am.	Some Rain. N.T.G.

1875 Wt. W593/826 1,000,000 4/15 J.B.C.&A. (A.D.S.S./Forms/C. 2118.)

No 2 Coy. 41st Divisional Train A.S.C.

WAR DIARY
or
INTELLIGENCE SUMMARY

(Erase heading not required.)

Army Form C. 2118

Instructions regarding War Diaries and Intelligence Summaries are contained in F. S. Regs., Part II. and the Staff Manual respectively. Title Pages will be prepared in manuscript.

Place	Date	Hour	Summary of Events and Information	Remarks and references to Appendices
RENINGHELST M.5.c.3.8 Sheet 28.	22.11.16		Reveille for Supply Section 3.30a.m. Remainder 5.30a.m. Stables 6-7. Railhead at WIPPENHOEK SIDING 11.15 to 12.15 and 3.30 - 4.30 p.m. followed by refilling. Other routine as before at 6.30 a.m.	fine
	23.11.16		Routine as above.	fine
	24.11.16		T4/057123 Dr. HARPER.T. T4/232193 Dr. SHAW.V. T4/094207 Dr TAYLOR.H. and T4/235281 Dr WILSON.J.E. reported here on transfer from No.1. Coy of the Train. T/22536 Dr CHIDGAY. H. admitted to 140 Field Ambulance. 1 Rider (No 3) shot.	fine
	25.11.16		Usual Routine. Supply details moved to WIPPENHOEK. Rider No 3 struck off strength.	Rain
	26.11.16		Usual Routine. T/22536 Dr CHIDGAY. H. discharged from 140 Fd FIELD AMBULANCE. Pte. JARMAN returned to 15th HANTS REGT. on completion of old shoeing course.	fair to wet
	27.11.16		Usual Routine. Pte. FLURRIE.C. joined from 122 M.G. Coy. for cold shoeing course.	fine

No 2 Coy. 41st Divisional Train ASC.

WAR DIARY
INTELLIGENCE SUMMARY

Army Form C. 2118

Place	Date	Hour	Summary of Events and Information		Remarks and references to Appendices
RENING HELST M/5.C.3.8 Sheet 28.	28.11.16		Usual Routine	S4/061261 a/Sergt. KEAR, W.A. admitted to 138 R. FIELD AMBULANCE	Cold and foggy	ASC
	29.11.16		Usual Routine	T/19687 a/Sergt. SCARRATT. F. T4/030751 Dr LE MARCHANT A.V. and T/23202 Dr MOORE A taken on strength of this Company.	Cold and foggy.	ASC
	30.11.16		Usual Routine.		Still.	ASC
						D A Galbraith Capt. Comdg No 2 Coy 41st Divnl Train

Army Form C. 2118

WAR DIARY or INTELLIGENCE SUMMARY

(Erase heading not required.)

No 2 Coy. 41st Divisional Train A.S.C.

Place	Date	Hour	Summary of Events and Information	Remarks and references to Appendices
RENINGHELST. M.5.c.3.8. Sheet 28.	1.12.16		Usual Company Routine viz:- Reveille 5.30 a.m. (3.30 a.m. for Supply Section.) Stables 6-7, 11.15-12.15, 4-5.15. Meals immediately after Stables. Lights out 9 pm. Railhead WIPPENHOEK SIDING 6.30 a.m. followed by Refill at same place. (L 28 d.3.8 Sheet 27)	Cold & dry
	2.12.16		Usual Routine as above. S4/061261 a/Sergt. KEAR W.A. transferred to A Coy. S4/064704 Pte. RUDLIN G.H. and S4/055823 Pte. McKAY. W. transferred to No1 Coy. S4/044398 a/Sergt. HALL G.F. transferred from No 4 Coy. S4/070722 Pte. SATTERTHWAITE W. " 1 " S4/070704 " JOHNSON W. " 3 "	ditto
	3.12.16		Usual Routine. 7/23202 Dr. MOORE A admitted to 140th. FIELD AMBULANCE	ditto
	4.12.16		Usual Routine	damp
	5.12.16		Usual Routine	Rain
	6.12.16		Usual Routine	Dull
	7.12.16		Usual Routine 7/23202 Dr. MOORE A evacuated to C.C.S. and struck off strength.	Fog.

No 2 Coy. 41st Divisional Train A.S.C.

WAR DIARY or INTELLIGENCE SUMMARY

Army Form C. 2118

(Erase heading not required.)

Place	Date	Hour	Summary of Events and Information	WEATHER	Remarks and references to Appendices
RENINGHELST M5.C.5.8 Sheet 28	8.12.16		Usual Routine. T/2/11241 Corpl. HASTINGS. D. transferred to No 4 Coy. T4/058109 Dr. BUTCHER W.H. " " "	Cold and damp	
	9.12.16		Company relieved of all transport work. Day devoted to foot drill squad drill and Commanding officers inspection.	Rain	
	10.12.16		Usual Routine.	Rain	
	11.12.16		Usual Routine. GEN. TOWSEY visited Refilling Point.	Cold & fine Rain later	
	12.12.16		Usual Routine. H.D. Horse No 86 sent to 52nd MOBILE VETERINARY SECTION and struck off strength. LIEUT. H.V. CUSACK struck off strength.	Snow and rain.	
	13.12.16		Usual Routine. T4/122791 Dr STEWART A.C. transferred from 4 Coy. T4/058109 " BUTCHER W.H. " to 4 Coy.	Rain	
	14.12.16		Usual Routine	Rain	
	15.12.16		Usual Routine. T4/13212 Sgt SPOUSE.R. admitted to 140th FIELD AMBULANCE LIEUT. C. TRIPP ASC transferred to 1 Coy. 2/LIEUT. H.N. PAGE ASC " " " 2 "	Fine	WSL

No 2 Coy 41st Divisional Train A.S.C.

WAR DIARY

(Erase heading not required.)

Army Form C. 2118

Instructions regarding War Diaries and Intelligence Summaries are contained in F. S. Regs., Part II. and the Staff Manual respectively. Title Pages will be prepared in manuscript.

Place	Date	Hour	Summary of Events and Information	Weather	Remarks and references to Appendices
RENINGHELST M.S.C.3.6 Sheet 28.	16.12.16		Usual Routine.	Fine	
	17.12.16		do	Fine	
	18.12.16		do	Fine	
	19.12.16		do	Snow	
	20.12.16		Reveille 5.15 am. Stables 5.45 - 6.45 Breakfast 6.45 Railhead 9.30. Rest of routine as before. COMMANDER-IN-CHIEF at RENINGHELST.	Dry and Cold	
	21.12.16		Routine as yesterday	Rain	
	22.12.16		do	Rain	
	23.12.16		do	Rain + gale	
	24.12.16		do	Dull	
	25.12.16		do Train two hours late at Railhead	High Wind	
	26.12.16		do GENERAL LAWFORD inspected horses.	Dull Rain late	
	27.12.16		do S4/065103 Pte McCARTHY.D. struck off strength on proceeding to England to take a Commission.	Bright and warm.	[signature]

No 2 Coy. 41st Divisional Train A.S.C.

WAR DIARY or INTELLIGENCE SUMMARY
(Erase heading not required.)

Army Form C. 2118

Place	Date	Hour	Summary of Events and Information	Remarks and references to Appendices	WEATHER
RENINGHELST M5.c.3.8. Sheet 28	28.12.16		Routine as yesterday. T/54031 a/Corpl. FINBOW. B.J. admitted to 140th FIELD AMBULANCE. T/3/024990 Dr. GAVAN. J. awarded 7 days F.P. No 1. and admitted to DETENTION CAMP.		Hard frost followed by showers at night.
	29.12.16		Routine as yesterday.		Rain gale
	30.12.16		Usual Routine. Refill one hour late.		Showery.
	31.12.16		Usual Routine. T2/13212 SGT. SPOUSE.R. proceeded to H.T. Base Drill.		

D.D. Galbraith Capt.
Comdg.

No. 2 COMPANY,
41st
DIVISIONAL TRAIN.
No.:
Date:

No 2 Coy. 41st Divisional Train

WAR DIARY or **A.S.C. INTELLIGENCE SUMMARY**
(Erase heading not required.)

Army Form C. 2118

Place	Date	Hour	Summary of Events and Information	WEATHER	Remarks and references to Appendices
RENINGHELST. M.5.c.3.8 Sheet 28.	1.1.1917.		Usual Routine, viz:- Reveille 5.30 a.m. Stables 6-7, 11.15-12.15, 3.30-4.45. Meals immediately after stables. Lights Out 9 p.m. 8.15 a.m. Railhead 9.30 followed by Refill at train side at WIPPENHOEK (L.28.d.3.8. Sheet 27). Now off to Railhead Strength of Company as per Daily State attached (Appendix I).	Fine	
	2.1.17		Usual Routine	Do	
	3.1.17		Company secured all duties. Day spent on extra grooming, harness and wagon cleaning. Baths. a/Corpl. FINBOW B.J. (T/24031) discharged from 140th FIELD AMBULANCE.	Fine and Cold	
	4.1.17		Usual Routine	Rain	
	5.1.17		Do	Fine	
	6.1.17		Do	Fine	
	7.1.17		Do	Rain	
	8.1.17		Do	Do	
	9.1.17		Do	Do	AA

Army Form C. 2118

No 2 Coy. 41st Divisional Train A.S.C.

WAR DIARY
or
INTELLIGENCE SUMMARY
(Erase heading not required.)

Instructions regarding War Diaries and Intelligence Summaries are contained in F. S. Regs., Part II. and the Staff Manual respectively. Title Pages will be prepared in manuscript.

Place	Date	Hour	Summary of Events and Information	Weather	Remarks and references to Appendices
RENINGHELST M.5.c.3.8. Sheet 28.	10.1.17		Usual Routine. One rider received from Remounts and taken on strength.	Showery and cold.	
	11.1.17		Do. Visited Veterinary fair at Reiding School.	Snow followed by rain	
	12.1.17		Do.	Do	
	13.1.17		Do.	Do	
	14.1.17		Do. One man proceeded on leave to England.	Frost + fog	
	15.1.17		Do. except that this Company's Refill from this date begins at 10 a.m.	Misty. Snow later	
	16.1.17		Do. T4/058569 Dvr ALDER A.E. proceeded to School of Cookery for a Course of Instruction	Slight Thaw	
	17.1.17		Do	Snow	
	18.1.17		Do	Still Thaw	
	19.1.17		Do	Still frosty	
	20.1.17		Do. except that from this date Refill at Railhead begins at 7.30 a.m.	Hard frost	
	21.1.17		Do. T4/036253 Dvr WILSON M transferred from Base (H T+S) Depôt and returned to 138th FIELD AMBULANCE. (as from 20th inst) Second Refill of Hay at 4 p.m. Inspection of horses by V.O.	Do	[signature]

1875 Wt. W593/826 1,000,000 4/15 J.B.C. & A. A.D.S.S./Forms/C. 2118.

WAR DIARY or INTELLIGENCE SUMMARY

Army Form C. 2118

No 2 Coy 41st Divisional Train A.S.C.

Instructions regarding War Diaries and Intelligence Summaries are contained in F.S. Regs., Part II. and the Staff Manual respectively. Title Pages will be prepared in manuscript.

(Erase heading not required.)

Place	Date	Hour	Summary of Events and Information	Remarks and references to Appendices
RENINGHELST M/5.C.3.8 Sheet 28.	22.1.17	Usual Routine		Hand post
	23.1.17	Do		do
	24.1.17	Do	T3/027003 Dr MURRAY M. discharged from Detention Camp	do
	25.1.17	Do	T/35519 Dr PERKIN R.W. admitted to 138th FIELD AMBULANCE. Train bat at Railhead (arrived 2 pm)	do
	26.1.17	Do		do
	27.1.17	Do	T4/235281 Dr WILSON J.E. admitted to 138th. FIELD AMBULANCE T/35519 Dr. PERKINS R.W. discharged from 140 H. "	do do
	28.1.17	Do	T/19687 a/SERGT. SCARRATT F. appointed a/COMPANY SERGEANT MAJOR. T3/023745 Dr YOXALL A. proceeded on Course of Instruction in Sanitary Duties.	do
	29.1.17	Do		do
	30.1.17	Do		do
	31.1.17	Usual Routine		do

D.S. Galbraith Capt
Comdg 2 Coy
41st Divisional Train
A.S.C.

1875 Wt. W593/826 1,000,000 4/15 J.B.C. & A. A.D.S.S./Forms/C. 2118.

WAR DIARY or INTELLIGENCE SUMMARY

Army Form C. 2118

No 2 Coy. 41st Divisional Train A.S.C.

Place	Date	Hour	Summary of Events and Information	WEATHER	Remarks and references to Appendices
RENINGHELST M/5. c.3.8 Sheet 28.	1.2.17		Usual Routine viz:- Reveille 5.30 a.m. Stables 6-7, 11.15-12.15, 3.30-5 p.m. (Supply Sections morning stable one hour earlier than above.) Meals immediately after stables. Lights out 9 p.m. Start for railhead on receipt of news that train has arrived (normally 6.15am) Railhead WIPPENHOEK, L.28.d.3.8, Sheet 27. Refill at train side. T/22538 Dr. CHIDGEY H. appointed a/L.Cpl. without pay, from 29.1.17.	Hard frost.	A.S.G.
	2.2.17		Usual Routine. T/030751 Dr. LE MARCHANT A.W. discharged from 140th FIELD AMBULANCE	Do	A.S.G.
	3.2.17		Do	Do	A.S.G.
	4.2.17		Do T/030751 Dr. LE MARCHANT A.W. to B.H.Q. for duty on 3rd inst to struck off strength from this date. Dr/ft. C.M.C. LUFF proceeded to A Coy. for duty (temporarily) S4/064854 a/Staff Sergt. MARSH J.J. proceeded to England for temporary Commission and is struck off strength.	Do	A.S.G.
	5.2.17		Usual Routine	Do	A.S.G.

No 2 Coy. 41st Divisional Train A.S.C.

WAR DIARY or INTELLIGENCE SUMMARY

Army Form C. 2118

Place	Date	Hour	Summary of Events and Information	Weather	Remarks and references to Appendices
RENINGHELST M.5.C.3.8 Sheet 28.	6.2.17		Usual Routine. T/20336 a/Farr. Sergt. PULLEN. H. appointed a/Farr. Staff Sergt with pay. T/8784 a/Sadd. Sergt WOODWARD.E.A. appointed a/Sdr. Staff Sergt without pay	Hard frost	SS4
	7.2.17		Usual Routine.	Do.	SS4
	8.2.17		Usual Routine.	Do.	SS4
	9.2.17		Usual Routine. T4/235281 Dr WILSON J.E. discharged from 140 H Field Ambulance.	Do	SS4
	10.2.17		Usual Routine. Relief very late (3.30 p.m.)	Do	SS4
	11.2.17		Do. T/36591 Dr DAVIS R.W. admitted to 138 H. Field Ambulance	Do	SS4
	12.2.17		Do.	Thaw	SS4
	13.2.17		Do. T/32536 a/Lcpl. CHIDGEY.H. appointed a/CPL with pay and transferred to 3 Coy. S4/070722 " SATTERTHWAITE W " " " " 4 "	Thaw Sunshine	SS4
	14.2.17		Do.	Do	SS4
	15.2.17		Do.	Cold & Snow	SS4
	16.2.17		Do.	Cold	SS4
	17.2.17		Do. G.O.C. inspected Camp. T/36591 Dr DAVIS R.W. struck off strength of Coy.	Some rain	SS4
	18.2.17		Do.	Cold	SS4
	19.2.17		Do.	Very Misty	SS4

WAR DIARY or INTELLIGENCE SUMMARY

(Erase heading not required.)

Army Form C. 2118

No 2 Coy 41st Divisional Train A.S.C.

Place	Date	Hour	Summary of Events and Information	Remarks and references to Appendices
RENINGHELST	20.2.17		Usual Routine, except that Refilling begins at 9.45 a.m. as from this date. Rain	SDG
M.S.C.3.8. Sheet 28	21.2.17		Do. Do.	SDG
	22.2.17		Do. Do.	SDG
	23.2.17		Do. T4/088565 Dr Greenlees J. found from Base (H.T. & S) depot and was transferred for transit to 138th Field Ambulance. Foggy	SDG
	24.2.17		Do. Dull	SDG
	25.2.17		Coy. excused all duties: in preparation for Marching Order Parade. Foggy	SDG
	26.2.17		Marching Order Parade and inspection of Company by Commanding Officer at 8 a.m. Usual Routine thereafter. T3/8966 Saddr-Dr Brady M admitted to 138 Field Ambulance. Fine	SDG
	27.2.17		Usual Routine. Cloudy; rain later	SDG
	28.2.17		Do. Still misty	SDG

D.D.T. Galbraith Capt.
OC 2 Coy. 41st Div Train.

Army Form C. 2118

WAR DIARY
or
INTELLIGENCE SUMMARY

(Erase heading not required.)

No 2 Coy. 41st Divisional Train ASC.

Instructions regarding War Diaries and Intelligence Summaries are contained in F.S. Regs., Part II. and the Staff Manual respectively. Title Pages will be prepared in manuscript.

Place	Date	Hour	Summary of Events and Information	Remarks and references to Appendices
RENINGHELST. M.5.c.3.8 Sheet 28.	1.3.17		Usual Routine viz:- Reveille 5:30 a.m. Stables 6-7, 11:15-12:15, 3:30-5 p.m. Meals immediately after stables. Lights out 9 p.m. Raihed WIPPENHOEK, L 28.d.3.8 Sheet 27 Refuse at traverse. 2nd Lieut. C.M.C. LUFF ASC and his servant T/35647 Dr. BRAID A. transferred to Train H.Q. T3/022987 A/Sergt. BULL. W. transferred from No 3 Coy.	Fine
	2.3.17		Usual Routine T3/8966 Sdr-Dr. BRADY. M. struck off strength as from 26.2.17	Fine
	3.3.17		Do.	Slight snow
	4.3.17		Do.	Cold Sleet
	5.3.17		Do.	Mild
	6.3.17		Do.	Cold + wry
	7.3.17		Do.	Very cold. Dry
	8.3.17		Do.	Slight snow
	9.3.17		Do.	Cold Sleet
	10.3.17		Do.	Mild
	11.3.17			Very mild

Army Form C. 2118

WAR DIARY
or
INTELLIGENCE SUMMARY
(Erase heading not required.)

N° 2 Coy 41st Divisional Train A.S.C.

Place	Date	Hour	Summary of Events and Information	Remarks and references to Appendices	WEATHER
RENINGHELST M 5.c.3.8. Sheet 28	12.3.17		Usual Routine		Mild
	13.3.17		Do. T4/124053 Whr-Corpl. WALKER S.G. returned to duty from Train H.Q.		Very Mild
	14.3.17		Do.		Mild. Rain
	15.3.17		Do.		Mild - Rain
	16.3.17		Do.		Mild - fine
	17.3.17		Do. T4/058084 Dr. SPARROW A.J.R. proceeded to England to take up temporary Commission and is struck off strength. 2/Lt PAGE A.S.C. struck off strength from 8.3.17		Fine
	18.3.17		Do.		Dull
	19.3.17		Do.		Dull. Rain
	20.3.17		Hours of Railhead changed to 7.45 a.m. Early parades for Supply section accordingly. Remainder of routine as usual. T5/144 Dr. SIMPSON C. } from Base H.T.&S. Depot and retransferred T1/5095 " NOBLE D. } to 138th. FIELD AMBULANCE. T2/017585 " WHITE G. } T/34122 Dr WALSH. T. } T/37215 " OVERTON C } Joined the Company from Base H.T.&S. Depot. T4/185437 Sdr. Dr. LUGG J.H. }		Very cold. Rain snow

No 2 Coy. 41st Divisional Train A.S.C.

WAR DIARY or INTELLIGENCE SUMMARY

Army Form C. 2118

Place	Date	Hour	Summary of Events and Information	Weather	Remarks and references to Appendices
RENINGHELST M5.c.38 Sheet 28	20.3.17 contd.		T3/027039 a/Sergt. ROBERTSON W.P. promoted SERGEANT T3/022987 " BULL W. " " T4/065307 a/Cpl. GREEN. F. " CORPORAL T4/065235 " EVERATT J.W. " " T4/058675 " BOLTON J.J. " " S4/042242 " BARON W. " " S4/070118 " NAISMITH A.N. " " S4/060467 a/L.Cpl. KINGS V.G. " L/CPL.		S.S.E.
	21.3.17		Routine as yesterday.	Rain. Cold.	S.S.E.
	22.3.17		Do T5/8393 Dr.S.S.M. TASKER W appointed a/FARR-CPL. without pay. T3/027805 Dr PARKER W appointed a/L-CPL with pay.	Snow and Rain	S.S.E.
	23.3.17		Do	Snow. Very cold	S.S.E.
	24.3.17		Do	Cold & fine	S.S.E.
	25.3.17		Do	Warm fine	S.S.E.

No. 2 Coy. 41st Divisional Train A.S.C.

WAR DIARY or INTELLIGENCE SUMMARY

Army Form C. 2118

(Erase heading not required.)

Instructions regarding War Diaries and Intelligence Summaries are contained in F.S. Regs., Part II. and the Staff Manual respectively. Title Pages will be prepared in manuscript.

Place	Date	Hour	Summary of Events and Information	Remarks and references to Appendices
RENINGHELST M 5.c.3.8 Sheet 28.	26.3.17		Usual Routine, but Supply Train late: four hours wait at Railhead.	ASG
	27.3.17		Do	ASG
	28.3.17		Do 21 N.C.Os and men awarded 1st Good Conduct Badge	ASG
			2 H.D. Horses (Nos. 64 & 85) sent to 52nd Mobile Veterinary Section. T4/122791 Dr. Stewart A.C. admitted to 140 R. Field Ambulance.	ASG
	29.3.17		Do	ASG
	30.3.17		Do	Showery	ASG
	31.3.17		Do	Showery	ASG

D S Galbraith Capt
O.C.

No 2 Coy. 41st Divisional Train A S C

WAR DIARY
INTELLIGENCE SUMMARY
(Erase heading not required.)

Army Form C. 2118

Place	Date	Hour	Summary of Events and Information	WEATHER	Remarks and references to Appendices
RENINGHELST M 15.c.3.8. Sheet 28.	1.4.17		Usual Routine, viz:- Reveille 5.30 Stables 6-7, 11.15-12.15, 3.30-5. Meals immediately after stables Lights out 9 p.m. Morning stables for Supply Section one hour earlier. Railhead WIPPENHOEK L.28.d.3.8. Sheet 27. Refill at Trainside. T/11334 Dr ELMSLIE G } from Base H.T. & S. depot taken on strength. S/290833 Pte WHITE D }	Dull	S.A.G.
	2.4.17		Usual Routine	Do	S.A.G.
	3.4.17		Do T/13938 Dr. BANNER N discharged from 139th Field Ambulance	Fine and cold.	S.A.G.
	4.4.17		Do T/36591 Dr. DAVIES R.W. returned from 3rd CANADIAN C.C.S. and taken on strength.	Light Rain	S.A.G.
	5.4.17		Do	Fine	S.A.G.
	6.4.17		Do Ten pairs sent to STEENVOORDE to bring back packs of 124 Brigade.	Rain	S.A.G.
	7.4.17		Do T/13938 Dr. BANNER N discharged from 139th Field Ambulance	Fine	S.A.G.
	8.4.17		Do	Fine cold.	S.A.G.

2 Coy. 41st DIVISIONAL TRAIN A.S.C.

WAR DIARY or INTELLIGENCE SUMMARY

Army Form C. 2118

Place	Date	Hour	Summary of Events and Information	WEATHER	Remarks and references to Appendices
RENINGHELST M5c38 Sheet 28	9.4.17		Usual Routine. S4/042242 Corpl. BARON. W. admitted to 138 K. FIELD AMBULANCE	Stormy	ADSS
	10.4.17		Do. 1 H.D. Horse No. 64 struck off strength.	Snow, fine intervals	ADSS
	11.4.17		Do.	Some snow	ADSS
	12.4.17		Do. OUDERDOM Shelled.	Fine. Cold. High Wind	ADSS
	13.4.17		Do. T/35591 Dr DAVIES R.W. with pair and wagon proceeded on detachment to Area Commandant BOESCHEPE.	Sunny. Dry. Cold wind.	ADSS
	14.4.17		Do. S4/042242 a/Corpl BARON W discharged from 139 K. FIELD AMBULANCE. 2Lt. C.M.C. LUFF } proceeded to TRAIN H.Q. T4/122791 Dr STEWART A.C. T/35647 Dr. BRAID A. } evacuated to 2nd CANADIAN C.C.S. and struck off strength	Sunny and dry. Cold wind.	ADSS
	15.4.17		Do. 1 Officer, 14 O.R., 2 Riders, 10 pairs and 10 G.S. Wagons all on strength of No 3 Coy. temporarily attached to this Coy. for rations.	Rainy	ADSS
	16.4.17		Do. T3/026231 Dr McNEE D. admitted to 138 K. FIELD AMBULANCE T4/122791 Dr STEWART A.C. discharged from 2nd CANADIAN C.C.S. and brought on strength again.	Sunny. Heavy rain later.	ADSS

WAR DIARY
INTELLIGENCE SUMMARY

(Erase heading not required.)

Army Form C. 2118

No 2 Coy. 41st Divisional Train ASC.

Instructions regarding War Diaries and Intelligence Summaries are contained in F.S. Regs., Part II. and the Staff Manual respectively. Title Pages will be prepared in manuscript.

Place	Date	Hour	Summary of Events and Information	WEATHER	Remarks and references to Appendices
RENINGHELST M5c.38. Sheet 28.	17.4.17	Usual Routine	T3/026231 Dr. M°NEE D. discharged from 138th FIELD AMBULANCE T4/058569 . ALLDER A.E. admitted to "	Very stormy Snow & Rain	ADG.
	18.4.17	Do	T4/058569 Dr ALLDER A.E. discharged from 138th FIELD AMBULANCE 1 Officer 12 OR. 2 riders and 10 pairs out of the details of 3 Coy. attached to this Coy. proceeded for duty with 4th SIEGE PARK.	Do	ADG.
	19.4.17	Do	T/11334 Dr ELMSLIE G. transferred to No 4 Coy. of TRAIN 2/Lt LOCHNER ASC T4/123823 Dr SAMPSON T.} posted to this Coy. from 4 Coy. C.F.	Dull & stormy Rain.	ADG.
	20.4.17	Hour of Railhead changed to 10 a.m. 5.45 - 6.45	Hours of nothing stables changed to Routine otherwise unaltered. T3/026982 a/Cpl I'ANSON C.F. reverts to permanent grade of driver (surplus to establishment of corporals)	Dull	ADG.
	21.4.17	Routine as yesterday.	T4/055913 Dr S. SMITH PHILLIPS F.G. posted to the Coy. from Base (H.T.(S) Depot.	Fine	ADG.
	22.4.17	Do	T/36497 Dr BODLEY G. transferred to 138th FIELD AMBULANCE	Do	ADG.

No 2 Coy. 41st Divisional Train A.S.C.

WAR DIARY
or
INTELLIGENCE SUMMARY
(Erase heading not required.)

Army Form C. 2118

Instructions regarding War Diaries and Intelligence Summaries are contained in F. S. Regs., Part II. and the Staff Manual respectively. Title Pages will be prepared in manuscript.

Place	Date	Hour	Summary of Events and Information	Weather	Remarks and references to Appendices
RENINGHELST M.5.c.3.8 Sheet 28.	23.4.17	Usual Routine	T/2/SR/02453 Dr KEEPING H., T/4/057521 Dr WOTHERSPOON D., 1 pair H.D. 1 pair Mules, 1 G.S. Wagon and 1 Limbered Wagon returned from detachment with Trench Warfare School. T/3/027103 Dr HUNTER P. 1 pair H.D. and 1 G.S. Wagon returned from detachment with 39th Road Repair Coy. T/36591 Dr DAVIES R.W., 1 pair H.D. and 1 G.S. Wagon returned from detachment with Area Commandant BOESCHEPE.	Fine	S.S.G.
	24.4.17	Do	Baggage pairs sent to Units.	Fine	S.S.G.
	25.4.17	H.Q. of Coy.	2 Officers 56 O.R. 10 Riders 9 H.D. and 5 mules proceeded by Route March with 122 INFANTRY BRIGADE at 9.7 am via ABEELE to billets at K34.C.5.8 (Sheet 27) en route for RECQUES TRAINING AREA. Distance 7 miles. Time occupied 5 hours. Supply wagons left c/o O.C. 3 Coy as supplies will be delivered by Motor Transport during training. 1 Officer. 15 O.R. 3 Riders and 18 H.D. detached for duty with 4th SIEGE COY. 1 O.R. left c/o O.C. 3 Coy in charge of 1 sick H.D. one sick mule. 1 Corporal left to hand over Canteen.	Dry and dull	S.S.G.

1875 Wt. W593/826 1,000,000 4/15, J.B.C. & A. A.D.S.S./Forms/C.2118.

No. 2 Coy. 41st Divisional Train A.S.C.

WAR DIARY
INTELLIGENCE SUMMARY

Army Form C. 2118

Place	Date	Hour	Summary of Events and Information	Weather	Remarks and references to Appendices
BEAUVOORDE K34.C.5.8 Sheet 27	26.4.17		Resting at BEAUVOORDE.	Very fine.	A.S.C.
	27.4.17		Proceeded at 8.30 a.m. by Route March with transport of Brigade via CASSEL to billets at RUBROUCK H.8.c.22 (Sheet 27) Distance 16 miles. Time 6¼ hrs including 2 hours midday halt near LE MENEGAT. Corporal Leff I/c Canteen at RENINGHELST rejoined. O.C. TRAIN visited Coy.	Dull	A.S.C.
RUBROUCK H.8.c.22 Sheet 27	28.4.17		Proceeded at 8.35 a.m. by Route March via BROXEELE, WULVERDINGHE WATTEN and EST MONT to billets at MONNECOVE. Distance 11 miles Time 7 hours including 1 hour's halt at WATTEN. Position of billets J.36.d.1.8 Sheet 27A. Proprietaire protested against our occupation of the dwelling house of the farm. Horses on lines. O.C. TRAIN visited Coy.	Very fine	A.S.C.
MONNECOVE J.36.d.1.8 Sheet 27A	29.4.17		Company rested. No duties. Horses exercised. Further protest from proprietaire.	Do.	A.S.C.
	30.4.17		Company Resting.		N.S. Galbraith Capt O.C. 2 Coy 41st Divisional Train A.S.C.

… Army Form C. 2118

WAR DIARY
or
INTELLIGENCE SUMMARY
(Erase heading not required.)

No 2 Coy. 41st Divisional Train A.S.C.

Place	Date	Hour	Summary of Events and Information	Weather	Remarks and references to Appendices
MONNECOVE J36.d.1.8. Sheet 27A			Supplementary to APRIL 1917.		
	28.4.17		2 H.D. Horses received at RENINGHELST from Remounts and taken on strength. Handed over to Lieut Shelton for duty with 4th Siege Coy.		A.T.G.
	30.4.17		7/13938 Dr. BANNER N admitted to 140th Field Ambulance. Baggage horses called in.		A.T.G.
			MAY. 1917.		
	1.5.17		H.Q. of Company (O.C. Coy. and A.A.O.R) resting at MONNECOVE. Daily routine as follows:- 5.45 a.m. Reveille. 6-7 Stables, water-up at farm. 9.30. Horses to exercise and water at J.26.c.7.6 (Sheet 27A) Between TOURNEHEM and ZOUAFQUES: distance 2¼ miles. 11-12 Stables. 12 noon Dinner. 2.30 Exercise and water as in morning. 4-5 Stables. Horses grazing at least one hour each day. 5pm Tea. 9pm Lights out. CAPT. H.M. MORRIS A.S.C. with Supply Details (9) and Loaders (9) are billeted at Railhead at WATTEN.	Brilliant Sunshine and warm.	A.T.G.
	2.5.17		Routine as yesterday	15°	A.T.G.
	3.5.17		Do	15°	A.T.G.
	4.5.17		Do O.C. TRAIN called.	15°	A.T.G.

WAR DIARY or **INTELLIGENCE SUMMARY**

Army Form C. 2118

No 2 Coy 41st Divisional Train ASC

Place	Date	Hour	Summary of Events and Information	Weather	Remarks and references to Appendices
MONNECOVE J36.d.1.8. Sheet 27A	5.5.17		Routine as yesterday. T4/057308 Dr ARMSTRONG RT. T4/235281 " WILSON J.E. T4/057256 " WALSHAW A. } proceeded to 2nd Army Rest Camp.	Brilliant sunshine warm	SS9
	6.5.17		Do. 2 Drivers and 4 mules of 1 Coy attached to 11th West Kents returned to this Coy.	Fine but colder	SS9
	7.5.17		Do.	Do	SS9
	8.5.17		Do. T/13938 Dr BANNER.N. discharged from 10th STATIONARY HOSPITAL and attached to No 3 Coy.	Fine and warm	SS9
	9.5.17		Do. Coy. fired 1000 rounds on miniature (30 yds) Range	Do	SS9
	10.5.17		Do. T4/055913 Dr.FARR. PHILLIPS F.J. proceeded to 2nd ARMY WORKSHOPS for temporary duty. NCOs on Map reading.	Do	SS9
	11.5.17		Do. NCOs on road reconnaissance	Fine and Very warm	SS9
	12.5.17		Do. T/36792 a/L. Co.H. KIRK. J. transferred to No. 4 Coy. Train. T/026737 L.Cpl. (a/Cpl) SAWDON.F. " " "	Do	SS9
	13.5.17		Do.	Do	SS9

No. 2. Coy. 41st Divisional Train A.S.C.

WAR DIARY
or
INTELLIGENCE SUMMARY
(Erase heading not required.)

Army Form C. 2118

Place	Date	Hour	Summary of Events and Information	Weather	Remarks and references to Appendices
MONNECOVE J 36 d 18 Sheet 27A	14.5.17		Routine as before. T/4/094207 Dr TAYLOR.H. awarded 1st G.C. Badge with Effect from 3.5.17. Baggage waggons to units.	Fine	A.D.S.T.
	15.5.17		Proceeded at 8 a.m. by Route March to RUBROUCK via WATTEN and BROXEELE where we occupied billets in FERME DE LA FOSSE. Distance 11 miles. Time 5 hrs. ¾ hour halt at top of WATTEN HILL.	do	A.D.S.T.
RUBROUCK H 8 C.22. Sheet 27	16.5.17		Proceeded at 6 a.m. by Route March with Brigade to BEAUVOORDE via LE MÉNÉGAT and NOORD PEENE (where we fed and watered) Distance 16½ miles. Time 6 hours. Same billets as outward journey. Two H.D. horses (Nos 25 and 89) sent to 52nd MOBILE VETERINARY SECTION from detachment at RENINGHELST.	Cloudy Cool Rain later.	A.D.S.T.
BEAUVOORDE M34.c.5.8. Sheet 27	17.5.17		Proceeded at 7.20 a.m. by Route March to RENINGHELST via ABEELE and POPERINGHE arriving at 12 noon. Distance 11 miles. Overjoyed camp vacated this day by 4 Coy. of Train. T/4/057123 Dr HARPER.T. transferred to No1 Coy of Train. Baggage waggons returned from units. 7 pairs H.D. 7 waggons 7 O.R. 1 WHR. CORPL and 1 4CPL attached from No 4 Coy.	Rain	A.D.S.T.

No 2 Coy. 41st Divisional Train A.S.C.

WAR DIARY or INTELLIGENCE SUMMARY

Army Form C. 2118

Place	Date	Hour	Summary of Events and Information	WEATHER	Remarks and references to Appendices
RENINGHELST	18.5.17		Back to normal Routine viz Reveille 5.30 Stables 6-7. 11.15-12.15, 4-5.15 Meals after Stables. Railhead 9 am. at WIPPENHOEK (L 28 d. 3. 8. Sheet 27) Refill at Railhead 10 am. 10 pairs on Stone Fatigue from DICKEBUSCH VOORMEZEELE at 9 pm. Lights out 9 pm. H.D. Horses Nos. 25 + 89 struck off strength.	Fine	S.L.C.
	19.5.17		Normal Routine	do	S.L.C.
	20.5.17		do	do	S.L.C.
	21.5.17		do 3 O.R. returned from 2nd Army Rest Camp 1 O.R. proceeded to " "	do	S.L.C.
	22.5.17		Normal Routine. No T/3/026982 Pte Samson C.F. reinstated in the appt of acting Corporal from 20th April 1917 inclusive	Dull some rain	O.C.Ms S
	23.5.17		Normal Routine	Very fine	O.C.Ms S
	24.5.17		Capt D.D. Galbraith proceeded on leave to England.	Very fine	O.C.Ms S
	25.5.17		Reveille 3 am Reveille point changed to Renninghelst Siding 9.21 to 7.1. Time of rising 6.30 am. Stables 3.30-4.30 am T/1196 B & at C.S.M Stonnaill T. and T4/057237 Dr Millar J proceeded on leave to England.	Very fine	O.C.Ms S

No 2 Coy. 41 Divisional Train A.S.C.

WAR DIARY or **INTELLIGENCE SUMMARY**

Army Form C. 2118

Place	Date	Hour	Summary of Events and Information	Weather	Remarks and references to Appendices
RENINGHELST	26.5.17		Normal Routine. T3/026982 Act/Cpl J'Anson C.7 forwarded to Base depot (HT&S) (Surplus to establishment)	Very fine	
	27.5.17		Normal Routine. Act c/s J'Anson Struck off the Strength on forwarding to Base depot. 2 H.D horses received from Remounts & brought on the Strength.	Do	
	28.5.17		Normal Routine	Do	
	29.5.17		Normal Routine T/34122 D/r Welch T admitted to 138 F.A. T4/094275 D/r Milburn D. Admitted to 58 F.A. Suffering from Shrapnel wounds received 29.5.17 & Struck off the Strength. (Died after admitted to F.A. 2P.M. 29*)	Fine	
	30.5.17		Normal Routine. No T/34122 D/r Welch T discharged from 29/12 C.C.S	Very fine	
	31.5.17		Railhead changed from G.21.d.7.1 to G.30.d.2.9 (sheet 28 NW) stables 5-6 a.m. Rifles 8 a.m. 6 H.D Lines (No 34) admitted to 5-2nd Mobile Vet. Section on A.D. allotted from 11 O R S returned to on Adm No 4 Coy & forwarded to England 11 O R allotted from No 40 labour Coy as loaders. T4/065218 D/r Hurst R.J. Brigade units on leave.	Very Fine	

From Skelton Lieut
O/C No 2 Coy 41 Div Train

Army Form C. 2118

WAR DIARY
or
INTELLIGENCE SUMMARY
(Erase heading not required.)

No. 2 Coy. 41st Divisional Train A.S.C.

Instructions regarding War Diaries and Intelligence Summaries are contained in F.S. Regs., Part II. and the Staff Manual respectively. Title Pages will be prepared in manuscript.

Place	Date	Hour	Summary of Events and Information	WEATHER	Remarks and references to Appendices
RENINGHELST G.34.b.6.6 Sheet 28.	1.6.17		Usual Routine viz:- Reveille 4.30 am. Stables 5-6 am., 11-12, 4-5.15 p.m. Meals immediately after Stables. Lights out 9 p.m. Railed OUDERDOM M.30.d.1.9 Sheet 28. Refilling on arrival of Pack Train, usually about 7.15 a.m.; this day at 12 noon. T2/SR.02453 Dr. KEEPING. H. proceeded to U.K. on leave.	Very fine.	A.S.G.
	2.6.17		Usual Routine	Do	A.S.G.
	3.6.17		Do. 7 pairs 7 G.S. wagons and 7 O.R. reattached to 4 Coy. This Coy was shelled out of camp at 6.15 p.m. and returned later. No casualties.	Do	A.S.G.
	4.6.17		Usual Routine T/35519 Dr PERKIN R.W. proceeded to BASE REST CAMP. T3/027039 Sgt. ROBERTSON W.P. returned from " T/34122 Dr WALSH. T. admitted to 138 H. FIELD AMBULANCE S4/070118 Cpl NAISMITH appointed a/Sgt with pay with effect from 28.4.17. Company moved to M.4.b.2.9. (Sheet 28): under canvas.	Do	A.S.G.

No 2 Coy. 41st Divisional Train A.S.C.

WAR DIARY or INTELLIGENCE SUMMARY

Army Form C. 2118

Place	Date	Hour	Summary of Events and Information	WEATHER	Remarks and references to Appendices
RENINGHELST M.4.b.29. Sheet 28.	5.6.17		Usual Routine. One H.D. horse (No.77) sent to Mobile Vet. Section (52nd.) T/34122 Dr WALSH T. discharged from 139th. FIELD AMBULANCE.	Very fine	A.D.Y.
	6.6.17		Usual Routine	Very fine	A.D.Y.
	7.6.17		do T/055913 Dr S.Sm. PHILLIPS F.J. returned from 2nd Army WORKSHOPS	Very fine. Showers at night	A.D.Y.
	8.6.17		do	do	A.D.Y.
	9.6.17		do	do	A.D.Y.
	10.6.17		do. One H.D (No.34) struck off the strength.	Dull Somewhat	O.C.M.S.
	11.6.17		do. One H.D. (No 45) received from Remounts and taken on the strength.	Dull and showery	O.W.M.S.
	12.6.17		Usual Routine. No T3/023745. Dr YOXALL A. admitted to 73rd FIELD AMBULANCE. One mule (No 90) transferred to No 3 COY A.S.C. One H.D. (No 77) received from the 52nd MOB. VET. SEC.	Very fine. Heavy thunder storm during evening	O.W.M.S
	13.6.17		Usual Routine. Coy moved to OUDERDOM (G.36.a.3.7.) T/065218 Dr HURST R.T. } Returned T/02453 Dr KEEPING.H. } to unit	Very fine.	O.W.M.S.
	14.6.17		do T/20236 A/FAR.S.SGT. PULLEN. H. proceeded on leave to ENGLAND.	Very fine	O.W.M.S.

WAR DIARY or INTELLIGENCE SUMMARY

Army Form C. 2118

No 2 Coy 41st Divisional Train A.S.C

Instructions regarding War Diaries and Intelligence Summaries are contained in F.S. Regs, Part II. and the Staff Manual respectively. Title Pages will be prepared in manuscript.

(Erase heading not required.)

Place	Date	Hour	Summary of Events and Information	Weather	Remarks and references to Appendices
OUDERDOM G.36.a.3.7	15.6.17		Normal Routine	Very fine	O.W.M.S
	16.6.17		Normal Routine. T3/023745 Dr YOXALL.A evacuated to No 2 CANADIAN C.C.S. 12.6.17 and struck off.	Very fine	O.W.M.S
	17.6.17		Refilling Point changed to WIPPENHOEK at 8AM. Reveillé 4.30 AM Stables 4.30 - 5.30. Transport moved off 6.30 A.M. C.O's inspection of camp and horses at 2.30 p.m.	Very fine	O.W.M.S
	18.6.17		Early réfée. 4 a.m. at WIPPENHOEK. T/23772 Dr COCKBURN.T and T4/083329 Dr TURNBULL R.H found from Base depot (H.T + S) and arranged on day strength. T/35519 Dr PERKIN R.W. returned from 2nd Army at camp.	Very fine heavy thunder storm during evening	O.W.M.S
	19.6.17		Normal Routine. Vicinity of camp shelled	Stormy	O.W.M.S
RENINGHELST (M.5.b.4.5)	20.6.17		Normal Routine. Coy moved to M.5.b.84 Sheet 28. T2/SR 03744 Dr Rudge A returned from leave.	Stormy	O.W.M.S
	21.6.17		Normal Routine. T4/055913 Dr S.S.M. PHILLIPS. F.J. returned to Base depot (H.T+S) Surplus to Establishment	Stormy	O.W.M.S
	22.6.17		Normal Routine. Company moved to G.34.C.74. Capt D.D.GALBRAITH. MacIjon Sick List 21.6.17. T3/027039 Sgt ROBERTSON. W.R. proceeded on Leave to England.	Stormy	O.W.M.S
(G.34.C.74.)	23.6.17		Normal Routine. Company moved to M.4 central. T4/055913 Dr S.S.M. Pt PHILLIPS struck off the strength	Fine	O.W.M.S
	24.6.17		Normal Routine. No casualties	Fine	O.W.M.S
	25.6.17		Normal Routine. Capt H Munro proceeded on leave to England	Fine Raining during evening	O.W.M.S

WAR DIARY or **INTELLIGENCE SUMMARY**

Army Form C. 2118

No 2 COY 41st DIVISIONAL TRAIN A.S.C.

Place	Date	Hour	Summary of Events and Information	WEATHER	Remarks and references to Appendices
RENINGHELST M4	26.6.17		Rolling point changed to RENINGHELST SIDING (G.27.d.74.) T/20336 a/Far. S. Sgt PULLEN. H returned from leave.	Fine.	OWMS
	27.6.17		Normal Routine. Capt. D.D.GALBRAITH evacuated to ENGLAND from No 14 GENERAL HOSPITAL on the 26 inst. Struck off the Strength. Lieut. O.W.M. SHELTON assumed command. (Temporary) Vice D.D.GALBRAITH. T2/SR.03744 Dr RUDGE.A admitted to 140 F.A. T3/027003 Dr MURRAY.M. admitted to 140 F.A. Baggage wagons of BAKERS, 11th RWKS. M.G.C. Sent to their units. Baggage & Supply wagons handed over to No 1 Coy	Fine	OWMS
R.32.d.9.5.	28.6.17		COY moved from RENINGHELST to R.32.d.9.5 by march route. Time taken 3½ hrs.	Stormy.	OWMS
	29.6.17		Rations dumped by lorries at 23.c.1.2. From thence taken by HT to units. T3/027003 Dr MURRAY discharged from 140 F.A.	Fine	OWMS
	30.6.17		Rained at CAISTRE at 11.45 A.M.	Wet.	OWMS

OWM Shelton Lieut
Comm'g No 2 Coy A.S.C.
41st Div'l Train

WAR DIARY or INTELLIGENCE SUMMARY

Army Form C. 2118

No 2 COY 41st DIVISIONAL TRAIN A.S.C.

Place	Date	Hour	Summary of Events and Information	WEATHER	Remarks and references to Appendices
Le Rouxlosmille R32d95.			Supplementary 15 JUNE 1917		
	30.6.17		2nd Lt. C.M.C. LUFF A.S.C. transferred from TRAIN HDQrs. 2nd Lt. C.F. LOCHNER A.S.C. transferred to TRAIN HDQrs as from 29.6.17		RSMS
			JULY 1917.		
	1.7.17		Supplies drawn from GAISTRE by motor lorries H.T. in bulk. Refilling Pt at XX C & 2. Baggage & Supply wagons of 18 K.R.R.S. detached to N0 1 Coy Train.	Dull	RSMS
	2.7.17		Normal Routine	Very fine	RSMS
	3.7.17		Normal Routine	Very fine	RSMS
	4.7.17		Normal Routine. T4/185437 Dr Sdr LUGG.I.H. proceeded to England on leave. INCO & one rider detached to 1 COY TRAIN in charge of 2nd line Transport of this unit.		RSMS
	5.7.17		Time of Stables whilst in Rest area altered. morning stables. 6.30 - 7.30 mid-day " 11.30 - 12.30 evening " 5. - 6.30 water & feed 9 p.m. One H.D. horse No 77 in charge of T3/027039 Sgt ROBERTSON. W.P. returned from leave. T2/SRO3744 Dr RUDGE.A. awarded to C.C.S. 27.6.17. and struck off the strength.	Very fine	
	6.7.17		Normal Routine. 2nd line transport of 12 E SURRY Regiment returned here.	Very fine	RSMS
	7.7.17		Normal Routine. Capt. H.M.T MORRIS returned from leave. One H.D. horse (No 46) died. Two pairs, pair G.S. wagons, one rider & 11 O.R. attached from No 1 Coy Train for 190 Bgde. R.F.A.	Very fine	RSMS

WAR DIARY
or
INTELLIGENCE SUMMARY

(Erase heading not required.)

Army Form C. 2118

No 2 COY 41ST DIVISIONAL TRAIN A.S.C.

Place	Date	Hour	Summary of Events and Information	WEATHER	Remarks and references to Appendices
LE ROUKLOSHILLE CR32d9.9	8.7.17		Normal Routine. T4/065235 CPL. EVERATT. J.W. admitted to 140 F.A. One H.D. horse No 46. Struck off the strength. Church parade at 5 P.M.	Showery	O.W.M.S
	9.7.17		Normal Routine. 1 H.D. horse (No 77) attached from No 1 Coy. wounded & struck off	Dull	O.W.M.S
	10.7.17		Normal Routine. 2nd line Transport of 18 K.R.R.S returned from unit.	Fine	O.W.M.S
	11.7.17		Normal Routine. Capt. E.M. WOOD. A.S.C. and 1 O.R. joined this unit	Very fine	O.W.M.S
	12.7.17		Tins of dripping at R4 & R6 at Rod Post closed up to 9 A.M. Refilling hand 11 A.M. Rewelded 4.30 Stables 5 A.M. - 6 A.M. 2nd line Transport of 15TH HANTS. returned from unit. Capt. E.M. WOOD. A.S.C. taken on the Strength from the 5th Cavalry Division A.S.C. and posted to this unit	Very fine	O.W.M.S
	13.7.17		Normal Routine. T/34215 Dr OVERTON. C. proceeded on leave to ENGLAND.	Very fine	O.W.M.S
	14.7.17		Normal Routine	Showery	O.W.M.S
	15.7.17		Normal Routine	Very fine	O.W.M.S
	16.7.17		Company Struck of duty for Shorts. TS/8393 L/Cpl TASKER W. proceeded on leave to ENGLAND. S4/055758 PTE HOWARD. A awarded Fine/good conduct badge which effect from 2.7.17.	Fine	O.W.M.S
	17.7.17		Normal Routine. g.o.c.s inspection at 3.30 P.M. T4/185437 Sddlr Dr LUGG. J.H. returned from leave.	Very fine	O.W.M.S
	18.7.17		Normal Routine. One H.D. horse No 24 sent to 52nd M.V.S. T4/065235 Cpl EVERATT. J.W. evacuated to 3rd Canadian C.C.S. 14th to in/out & Struck of the Strength from that date, 2nd line Transport 228 Coy. R.E sent to unit.	Showery	O.W.M.S

No. 2 COY 41ST DIVISIONAL TRAIN A.S.C.   R32.d.9.5.   Army Form C. 2118

WAR DIARY
or
INTELLIGENCE SUMMARY
(Erase heading not required.)

Instructions regarding War Diaries and Intelligence Summaries are contained in F.S. Regs., Part II. and the Staff Manual respectively. Title Pages will be prepared in manuscript.

Place	Date	Hour	Summary of Events and Information	WEATHER	Remarks and references to Appendices
LE ROUKLESHILLE AREA. R32.d.9.5.	19.7.17		Normal Routine.	Fine	OWMS
	20.7.17		Normal Routine. Callow E.M. WOOD having joined this Company on the 10th inst. appointed Command from that date.	Fine	OWMS
	21.7.17		Normal Routine. One H.D. Horse (No.24) evacuated 19.7.17. and struck off the Strength. T4/057534 Dr. McNAMA O admitted to 140 F.A. 2nd Line Transport of 190 Bgde. RFA returned to No.1 Coy Train. 5 hrs. S.G.S. wagons & 12 other ranks attached from No.1 Coy Train.	Very fine	OWMS
	22.7.17		Normal Routine. No T1/4820 Dr MEAGHER P joined the Coy from Base depot & taken on the Strength.	Very fine	OWMS
M.17 a Cnt.d	23.7.12		Company moved by route march to M.17 a Cent.d. Time occupied 3½ hrs. Feeding at Railhead during Lomis. Horses refusing ht to new camp. Supplies conveyed by H.T. T3/024490 Dr. GAVIN J admitted to 138 F.A. T/36565 Dr DEAN A.H. warned to C.C.S. 12 inst. struck off the Strength.	Very fine	OWMS
M.11 C.4.8.	24.7.17		Rations at M.11 C.48 at 12.30 P.M. Supplies conveyed by motor transport to Dump. Thence by H.T. to units. Coy moved to M.11.C.4.8.	Very fine	OWMS
	25.7.17		Railhead at BRULOZE 9.15 A.M. Refuel in camp at 11 AM.	Very wet	OWMS
	26.7.17		Time of feeding from railhead altered to 9 A.M. T/37215 Dr. OVERTON C. returned from leave.	Fine	OWMS
	27.7.17		Normal routine. No Casualties	Fine	OWMS
	28.7.17		Normal routine. T5/8893 A/T/Cpl. TASKER W. returned from leave.	Very fine	OWMS

No 2 COY 41st DIVISIONAL TRAIN A.S.C.

WAR DIARY or **INTELLIGENCE SUMMARY**

Army Form C. 2118

M II C 4 8. (Sht 28 S.W.)

Place	Date	Hour	Summary of Events and Information	Weather	Remarks and references to Appendices
M II C 4 8.	29.7.17		Normal routine T3/02449 Dr GAVIN J. evacuated to No 11 C.C.S. 24.7.17 and struck off the strength. 2 O.R. proceeded to 2nd Army. Not cas'y.	Very wet	O.S.M.S.
	30.7.17		Normal routine. T4/083329 Dr TURNBULL R.H. transferred to 138 Field Ambulance for duty. T4/237948 Sgt BREWER C. and T/329887 Dr HARRIS M. joined from Base Depot & returned posted to 138 Fld Amb for duty.	Wet	O.S.M.S.
	31.7.17		Normal Routine.	Dull	O.S.M.S.

C.W.M. Shelton Lieut.
N°. 2 Coy A.S.C.
41st Divisional Train

No 2 COY. 41st DIVISIONAL TRAIN A.S.C.   M11C.4.8.

WAR DIARY or INTELLIGENCE SUMMARY
(Erase heading not required.)

Army Form C. 2118

Instructions regarding War Diaries and Intelligence Summaries are contained in F.S. Regs., Part II. and the Staff Manual respectively. Title Pages will be prepared in manuscript.

Place	Date	Hour	Summary of Events and Information	Weather	Remarks and references to Appendices
M11C.4.8.	1.8.17		Normal Routine	Very wet.	RWW
	2.8.17		Normal Routine. 2nd Lieut C.M.C. LUFF posted to No 1 Coy. Train.	Very wet	RWW
	3.8.17		Normal Routine. One H.D. horse (No 33) failed by Shrapnel & Struck off.	Very wet.	RWW
	4.8.17		Normal Routine. T4/058569 Dr ALDER A.E. returned from leave. T4/067534. Dr MACNAMA. O. discharged from 9th Field Amb. T/343220 Dr BARTRAM. T, T4/251665. Dr BROWN R.M., T/14033 Dr BALL E, T/1896 Dr BAKER. P. joined from Base depot. T/1896 Dr BAKER. P. returned to 138 F.A. for duty. 2 H.D. horses received from remounts.	Very wet	RWW
	5.8.17		Refilling Point changed to M17C.6.5. NO.T/367753 Dr FINCH. G.W. forfeits Good Conduct badge as from 28.7.17	Fine	RWW
	6.8.17		Railhead changed to BAILLEUL. On riding No. 13. transferred to 2nd Army remount Section, and Struck off. NoT4/090354 A/cpl CHASE H.B. joined from Base depot. T4/144227 Dr FOWLER E.W. and T/308998 Dr YEOMANSON. W.C. joined from Base depot. and returned to 138 F.A. for duty.	Fine	RWW
	7.8.17		Normal Routine. One H.D. horse (No 93) Sent to 52nd Mobile Vet Sec.	Very fine	RWW
	8.8.17		Time of refilling altered to 8 AM	Fine.	RWW
	9.8.17		Time of refilling altered to 9 AM. T4/159682 Dr WOODHOUSE. P. returned to 5th CAVALRY Divisional A.S.C.	Fine	RWW
	10.8.17		Normal Routine. Riding horse No 13 on charge to this Coy. reclassified as a draft horse due to this company no form of unclad	Fine	RWW

No 9 Coy 41st DIVISIONAL TRAIN
A.S.C.

WAR DIARY or INTELLIGENCE SUMMARY

Army Form C. 2118

(Erase heading not required.)

Instructions regarding War Diaries and Intelligence Summaries are contained in F.S. Regs, Part II. and the Staff Manual respectively. Title Pages will be prepared in manuscript.

Place	Date	Hour	Summary of Events and Information	WEATHER	Remarks and references to Appendices
M11.c.3.8	11.8.17		Railhead changed to BRULOOZE. Time of filling 9.15 A.M.	Very Stormy	OMS
	12.8.17		Time of filling at Railhead changed to 10.15 A.M. T4/198191 Dr JONES. S.G. T4/251668 Dr BROWN. R.M. awarded 1st First G.C. Proceeded to rest camp. Rest camp Lodge	Stormy	OMS
	13.8.17		Normal Routine. S4/070116 Q/Sgt NAISMITH. A.N. Proceeded on leave. T3/026231 Dr McNEE. D returned from leave. T5/18951 A.Sddlr c/r JOBSON. T.E and S4/056882 Pte SMITH. H.T. returned from rest camp. T/Lieut G.W GREY joined from Base depot and attached to this Company. Baggage & wagons sent to Brigade units.	Fine	OMS
Reg.d.5.2 Sh 27 S.E.	14.8.17		Refilling as usual. then Coy moved to R19. d 5 2.	Showery	OMD
	15.8.17		Railhead changed to BAILLEUL. Time of filling 9.15 A.M.	Very Stormy	OMS
	16.8.17		Normal Routine. No casualties	Very fine	OMS
	17.8.17		Two heavy Draft horses received from Remounts. One rider No 2 sent to Remounts as surplus to establishment. Normal Routine	Very fine	OMS
	18.8.17		Normal Routine	Very fine	OMS
	20.8.17		Company moved by route march to LE NIEPPE distance 19 kilometres. Time occupied 5 hrs arriving in camp. G/L. moved to refilling point & divisibles returns to units	Very fine	OMD
	21.8.17		Company moved to ACQUIN area Sht 27A. V16.c.5.0. Supplies drawn by M.T. from ST OMER & brought to V4.c.8.3. H.T. delivered to units. Time of refilling 12 Noon.	Very fine	OMS
	22.8.17		Normal Routine. Same as 21.8.17. T4/057308 Dr ARMSTRONG. R.T. Proceeded on leave	Very fine	OMS

No. 2 Coy 41st Div. TRAIN A.S.C.   V.16 a k.o

WAR DIARY or INTELLIGENCE SUMMARY

Army Form C. 2118

(Erase heading not required.)

Instructions regarding War Diaries and Intelligence Summaries are contained in F.S. Regs., Part II. and the Staff Manual respectively. Title Pages will be prepared in manuscript.

Places	Date	Hour	Summary of Events and Information	Weather	Remarks and references to Appendices
ACQUIN V.16 a & 0	23.8.17		Normal Routine. Supply, Horsed baggage + Pd 4ms at Acquin in the vicinity	Stormy	Nil
	24.8.17		Normal Routine. Acquin & vicinity in the vicinity	Fine	Nil
	25.8.17		Normal Routine	Fine	Nil
	26.8.17		Normal Routine	Fine. Heavy rain at night	Nil
	27.8.17		Normal Routine. Supply wagons of 190 Bde. R.F.A. Ammo D. Batt. attached from No 1 Coy. Train	Very wet	Nil
	28.8.17		Normal Routine. All members of the Coy examined by Advice of horse mass brght of 10th Corps for hostile purposes	Very Stormy	Nil
	29.8.17		Normal Routine	Very Stormy	Nil
	30.8.17		Time of Reveille changed to 9 A.M.	Stormy	Nil
	31.8.17		Time of Reveille changed to 8.30 A.M.		

SWM Shelton Lieut.
2/o Y. A.S.C.
41st Div. Train.

No 2 COY 41ST DIV TRAIN A.S.C.

WAR DIARY
INTELLIGENCE SUMMARY
(Erase heading not required.)

Army Form C. 2118

Instructions regarding War Diaries and Intelligence Summaries are contained in F.S. Regs., Part II. and the Staff Manual respectively. Title Pages will be prepared in manuscript.

Place	Date	Hour	Summary of Events and Information	WEATHER	Remarks and references to Appendices
ACQUIN	1.9.17		Normal Routine.	Stormy	Sund
VIEQ a SO.	2.9.17		Normal Routine	Fine	Sund
Shd 27 A.S.E	3.9.17		Normal Routine	Very fine	Sund
	4.9.17		Normal Routine. Supply wagons of 190 Bde R.F.A & 2 D Battery returned to units for issue.	Very fine	Sund
	5.9.17		Normal Routine. One O.R transferred to 138 F.A for duty & Struck off Company Roll. B.H.Q at cricket.	Very fine	Berk S.
	6.9.17		Normal Routine. One O.R returned from Course.	Fine. rain at night	Ph/M S.
	7.9.17		Normal Routine. 2 O.R.s returned from rest camp.	Dull.	Sund.
	8.9.17		Normal Routine. Coy Royal enabled motor against Ranters. won.	Very fine	Berk.
	9.9.17		Normal Routine. 2 O.R Joins from Base depot & retransferred to 138 F.A. 2 O.R taken on the Strength.	Very fine	Berks S.
	10.9.17		Normal Routine	Very fine	P/M S
	11.9.17		Normal Routine	Very fine	P/M S
	12.9.17		Normal Routine. No Coy Royal B.H.Q at cricket won	Very fine	Proms S
	13.9.17		Normal Routine. Baggage wagons sent to Brigade units for move to ENGLAND.	Dull.	Sund
LE NIEPPE	14.9.17		Coy travel by route march to LE NIEPPE N 34. a. 5.o. Supply wagons travelled loaded after arrival distributed to units. 2nd Rifle of LE NIEPPE from Rouen	Very fine	Sund.
MONT D.E.CATS	15.9.17		Coy entrained march to MONT DE CATS. R.19. d. 54 (Sheet 27 S.E) Supply wagons travelled no day transport. Rifles in camp that evening to distributing to units.	Very fine	Sund.
	16.9.17		C.O.Y entrained march to N 19.76. Sheet 28 S.W. on H.Q line No 79 Loing died 14.9.17 Struck off. 3 O.R Joins from Base depot to address Cateroany A class.	Very fine	Sund.

1875 Wt. W593/826 1,000,000 4/15 J.B.C. & A. A.D.S.S./Forms/C. 2118.

No. 2 COY 41ST DIVISIONAL TRAIN A.S.C.

N1076.

WAR DIARY

INTELLIGENCE SUMMARY

(Erase heading not required.)

Army Form C. 2118

Instructions regarding War Diaries and Intelligence Summaries are contained in F. S. Regs., Part II. and the Staff Manual respectively. Title Pages will be prepared in manuscript.

Place	Date	Hour	Summary of Events and Information (H3a 4.2.1.)	WEATHER	Remarks and references to Appendices
N1a 76	17.9.17		Railroad OUDERDOM Siding at 9 a.m. refilling in camp. Supply wagon of 62 M.G.C. Joined from 21st Divisional Train	Fine	Burnd
	18.9.17		Normal Routine. T4/065307 C/a GREEN F. admitted to 139. FA	Dull	Burn S.
	19.9.17		Normal Routine. 3 O.R. (attaq ory a chelon) transferred to Base depot & struck off strength	Fine	Burnd
	20.9.17		Normal Routine	Fine	Burnt
	21.9.17		Normal Routine. 2nd Lieut. S.G. ALDOUS. A.S.C. joined from Bam Depot. 19.9.17 posted to div comp	very fine	Burnd
	22.9.17		Normal Routine. Capt. E.M. WOOD. A.S.C. proceeded to ENGLAND on leave. Lieut. D.W.M. SHELTON assumed temporary command of the Coy. Baggage wagons attached to units	fine	Burnt
	23.9.17		Coy moved by route march to CAESTRE Area W2.C 2.2. Train occupied above ground. Supply wagons travelled loaded. Refill at 10 AM. after delivery in evening.	very fine	Burnd
CAESTRE W2C22	24.9.17		Railhead at CAESTRE at 9 AM. Refilling at 10 AM in camp	very fine	Burnt
	25.9.17		Normal Routine. T4/065307 C/M GREEN F. evacuated to C.C.S. 21.9.17 Struck off strength.	very fine	Burnt.
I6c9.20(KF17)	26.9.17		Coy moved. WORMHOUDT I6c92 Supply travelled looked. No delivery	fine	Burnd
J2a22(SLt 17)	27.9.17		Coy moved to GHYVELDE J2a 2.2. One O.R. returned from leave. Supply wagons delivered Later refilled from limins in camp.	very fine.	Burnd
WI5.6.3.9. (SLT 11)	28.9.17		Coy moved to LA PANNE WI5.6.3.9. SLtr. Supply wagons delivered & refilled a second time.	very fine	Burnt.
	29.9.17		Railroad at ADINKERKE at 9.30 A.M. Baggage wagons returned from units. 4 O.R.S. proceeded to ENGLAND on leave.	very fine	Burnd
	30.9.17		Normal Routine	very fine	Burn S.

Cum Shelton Lt.
O.C. No 2 Coy A.S.C.
41st Div Train

WAR DIARY
or
INTELLIGENCE SUMMARY

(Erase heading not required.)

Army Form C. 2118

Instructions regarding War Diaries and Intelligence Summaries are contained in F. S. Regs., Part II. and the Staff Manual respectively. Title Pages will be prepared in manuscript.

Place	Date	Hour	Summary of Events and Information	Remarks and references to Appendices
LA PANNE W/5 b 3.9 Sheet 11	1/10/17		LIEUT O.W.M. SHELTON proceeded to England for instruction for Infantry statis on 30.9.17 and struck off the strength. LIEUT C. TRIPP (act Capt.) assumes temporary command of this Coy. Refill ADINKERKE at 9.30 a.m. Second line transport of 19th Middlesex Reg joined on attachment from No 7 boy train. One O.R. proceeded on leave. Weather wet rain.	C.T.
do	2/10/17		Normal Routine No 1/30391 Dr SCROGGIE. C. admitted to 138 Field Ambulance. Weather very fine	C.T.
do	3/10/17		Normal Routine. Four Other Ranks proceeded on Leave. Two O.R. Transferred to John H.Q. Two O.R. Transferred from train H.Q. Weather dull	C.T.
do	4/10/17		Normal Routine. Weather Wet	C.T.
do	5/10/17		Normal Routine. Supplies drawn in bulk from Railroad. One other Rank proceeded on leave. No 1/30391 Dr SCROGGIE. C. Brigade evacuated to C.C.S. and struck off. Weather dull	C.T.
do	6/10/17		Normal Routine. Baggage wagons sent to units for more (cancelled) LIEUT GREY.G.W. proceeded on leave. Weather stormy	C.T.

Army Form C. 2118

WAR DIARY
or
INTELLIGENCE SUMMARY
(Erase heading not required.)

Instructions regarding War Diaries and Intelligence Summaries are contained in F.S. Regs, Part II. and the Staff Manual respectively. Title Pages will be prepared in manuscript.

Place	Date	Hour	Summary of Events and Information	Remarks and references to Appendices
LAPANNE	7.10.17		Coy moved to W 18 a 2.5 Sheet 11 ZEEPANNE supplies drawn from Railhead 6.10.17 delivered. No refill owing to no drays reservation being employed. Infty Railhead changed to ST. IDESBALD (light Railway) at W 17 B 5.15. Weather Wet	C.J.
ZEEPANNE	8.10.17		Refill at 9 am 2 HD horses attached from No 1 Coy. Train sent to 52 M.V.S. Baggage wagons returned from their. Weather Wet	C.J.
do	9.10.17		Refill at 8.15 am No 1/26301 a/Bpl LORIMER.F. joined from Base depot and taken on the strength. Weather dull	C.J.
do	10.10.17		Normal Routine Weather dull	C.J.
do	11.10.17		Refill 7.0 am Four other Ranks proceeded on leave. Two HD horses Nos 49 & 19 evacuated on the 9th and struck off Weather fine	C.J.
do	12.10.17		Normal Routine Weather Stormy	C.J.
do	13.10.17		Normal Routine 2 HD Horses arrived from Remounts 4 Other Ranks returned from leave 1 Other Rank proceeded on leave. Weather very wet	C.J.
do	14.10.17		Normal Routine Weather fine	C.J.
do	15.10.17		Normal Routine 1 HD Horse No 66 sent to 52 M.V.S. Weather fine	C.J.

WAR DIARY or INTELLIGENCE SUMMARY

Army Form C. 2118

(Erase heading not required.)

Instructions regarding War Diaries and Intelligence Summaries are contained in F.S. Regs., Part II. and the Staff Manual respectively. Title Pages will be prepared in manuscript.

Place	Date	Hour	Summary of Events and Information	Remarks and references to Appendices
ZEEPANNE W19 A 2.5 Sheet 11	16.10.19		Normal Routine. 4 other Ranks proceeded on leave. 10 other Ranks returned from leave. Weather dull.	C.T.
do	17.10.19		Normal Routine. Lt G.W. GREY returned from leave. Weather fine.	C.T.
do	18.10.19		Normal Routine. 2nd line transport of 19th Middlesex Reg. returning to do I do train tour other Ranks returned from leave of Weather.	C.T.
do	19.10.17		Normal Routine. 1 H.D. Stores no 66 evacuation 15 other ranks evacuated off. Weather strong.	C.T.
do	20/10/19		Normal Routine. S/Mjr. 10800 g. D.H.Q. joined on attachment from No.1 Coy train. S6-904 Sergt Monteith. W.B. joined from Base depot. Weather fine.	Q. w.g
do	21/10/19		Normal Routine from O.R. proceeded on leave - T4 - 244592 L. Cpl. Evans. A.M. transferred from No 4 Cy train. Weather fine.	Q. w.g
do	22/10/19		Normal Routine. Weather fine.	Q. w.g
do	23/10/19		Normal Routine. Capt. (Brevt Major) A.L. Mackay A.S.C. joined from Base depot - T. attached to No 2 Coy train. Capt.&M. Wood A.S.C. returned from leave. Weather wet.	Qw.g
do	24/10/19		Normal Routine. 1 F.B. received from Bourmonte. 3 O.R. returned from leave. weather fine.	Q. w.g
do	25/10/19		Normal Routine. S/35557.3 Pte Hacking F. transferred to No 5 Coy train. 1 O.R. returned from leave. Weather dull.	Q. w.g
do	26/10/19		Normal Routine. Weather fine.	Q.w.g
do	27/10/19		Normal Routine. Weather fine.	Q.w.g

Army Form C. 2118

WAR DIARY
or
INTELLIGENCE SUMMARY
(Erase heading not required.)

Instructions regarding War Diaries and Intelligence Summaries are contained in F. S. Regs., Part II. and the Staff Manual respectively. Title Pages will be prepared in manuscript.

Place	Date	Hour	Summary of Events and Information	Remarks and references to Appendices
ZEEPANNE W18a2.5 Sheet 11	28/10/17		Normal Routine. Baggage waggons sent to trails for move. 1 O.R. returned from leave.	July
	29/10/17		Coy moved by road route to COUDEKERQUE BRANCHE H11c5.5 Supply waggons handed over supplies & returned with units after delivery. Sent to 52 M.V.S. Weather fine.	1 H.D. Q.W.Q.
COUDEKER -QUE BRANCHE H11c5.5	30/10/17		Refill in Camp at 10.0 A.M. Weather. Raining. 4 O.R. from leave.	Q.W.Q.
Do	31/10/17		Normal Routine. Weather fine.	Q.W.Q.

Fulwood........ CAPTAIN,
O.C. No. 2 COY. 41st DIVISIONAL TRAIN

WAR DIARY
or
INTELLIGENCE SUMMARY

(Erase heading not required.)

Army Form C. 2118

Instructions regarding War Diaries and Intelligence Summaries are contained in F. S. Regs., Part II. and the Staff Manual respectively. Title Pages will be prepared in manuscript.

Place	Date 1918	Hour	Summary of Events and Information	Remarks and references to Appendices
S MARTINO (ITALY)	March 1		Coy HQ marched at 3 am to FONTINEVA and entrained 8 am. T/34122 Dr WALSH. T. evacuated to No 24 C.C.S. on 25th Feb-18 and struck off. Weather wet.	G.T.
	2		Train journey	R.T.
	3		Train journey	G.T.
	4		Coy H.Q. detrained at DOULLENS (FRANCE) at 4 pm and marched to POMMERA. Weather damp	G.T.
POMMERA Dept France LENS II 4F 20.15	5		No refill. Weather fine	R.T.
	6		No refill. T4/251665 Dr BROWN. R.M. admitted to 138 Field Ambulance. Weather fine	G.T.
	7		No refill. Lieut G.W. GREY A.S.C. transferred to No1 Coy. Train 2 wd Lieut P.R.L. SAVILL a S.C. joined from 2nd A.S.C. Base depot and posted to this Coy. Weather fine	G.T.
	8		Part refill. Bread meat and potatoes. Baggage and supply wagons rejoined from unit. T1/090354 left CHASE. H.P. admitted to 138 F.A. Weather fine.	G.T.
	9		Refill at Coamp at 10 am from Lorries. Weather fine	G.T.

WAR DIARY
or
INTELLIGENCE SUMMARY

(Erase heading not required.)

Army Form C. 2118

Instructions regarding War Diaries and Intelligence Summaries are contained in F. S. Regs., Part II. and the Staff Manual respectively. Title Pages will be prepared in manuscript.

Place	Date 1918	Hour	Summary of Events and Information	Remarks and references to Appendices
POMMERA Lieu FRANCE	10	noon	Refill as usual & CAPT H.M. MORRIS and 4 OR proceeded on leave. Weather fine	L.J.
LENS II 4F 20.15	11	"	Refill as usual. Supply wagons of St HQ Signals, 199 M.G.C. and C RE returned to camp. Tn/0 90354 left CHASE H.P evacuation to C.C.S. on 9th amb anor. struck off. Weather fine	L.J.
	12	"	Refill at 9.30 am Weather fine	L.J.
	13	"	Normal routine 5 OR proceeded on leave. Weather fine	L.J.
	14	"	Normal routine 74/251665 Pte BROWN. R.M. evacuated to No 3 San. Sect. Light. M 4 ambce and struck off. HD 84 admitted to M.V.S. T4/065298 Pte COTTON F. from No 1 Coy to No Resy. T2/SR04453 Pte KEEPING. H. from No 2 to No 1 Coy O.C. inspected 1st line transport of 122 Inf Bde. Weather fine.	L.J. 1
	15	"	Normal Routine Weather fine	L.J.
	16	"	Normal Routine 6 OR returned from leave. Weather fine	L.J.
	17	"	Normal Routine 1 HD No 84 evacuated from M.V.S. M 15th anal struck off. Supply wagons of 122 & 199 MGC & joined their respective units. Weather fine	L.J.
	18	"	Refill at 9.30 am and ammor refill at 3 pm Wagons rejoined. Weather fine	L.J.
	19	"	Rations delivered. Refill at 1.30 p.m. T/23419 Dr HILTON. E. transferred from No 1 Coy to am. Weather wet.	L.J.

Army Form C. 2118

WAR DIARY
INTELLIGENCE SUMMARY
(Erase heading not required.)

Instructions regarding War Diaries and Intelligence Summaries are contained in F. S. Regs., Part II. and the Staff Manual respectively. Title Pages will be prepared in manuscript.

Place	Date	Hour	Summary of Events and Information	Remarks and references to Appendices
POMMERA *Que France* LENS 11 4F 20.15	20	Noon	Refill arrived. Coy marched to FORCEVILLE and delivered supplies in new area. 10 R returned from leave. Weather dull	B.J.
FORCEVILLE LENS 11	21	.	Coy marched to RIBEMONT refill. Am Supply Column for consumption 23rd I.H.D No 94 destroyed 20 mins and turned off. Weather fine	B.J.
RIBEMONT AMIENS	22		Coy marched to ACHIET-LE-PETIT at 9 h 15 with horse line transport. At ALBERT arrived at 3 h m delivered supplies in new area to Regiment from Base depot and brought in the strength. Weather fine	B.J.
ACHIET-LE-PETIT 23 LENS 11	23		Refill arrived. Lorries at 11 am and delivered 2 Lt P.R.L. SAVILL A.S.C. admitted to 138 Field ambulance. Weather fine	B.J.
	24		Refill from Lorries at 9 am and delivered. Supply wagons arrived. Refill from MIRAUMONT Railhead and refilled in south for lorries 25th. 2 H D horses and two G S wagons travel with supplies destroyed by shell fire 4 hours 12 and 13 TH/0949 2. Lt BRIDSON. R.D. attached from the 6 Dn. was wounded by shell fire and admitted to 138 Field Ambulance. Coy marched to E of BUCQUOY at 6 p.m. Weather fine	B.J.
BUCQUOY	25		Coy marched at 3:15 am to BIENVILLERS delivered supplies. Coy marched at 3 h m to ST AMAND. Weather fine.	B.J.
ST AMAND	26		Refill from Lorries at 9:0 am Coy marchy to WH of BAILLEUVAL and delivered supplies. Weather fine	B.J.

1875 Wt. W593/826 1,000,000 4/15 J.B.C. & A. A.D.S.S./Forms/C. 2118.

WAR DIARY
INTELLIGENCE SUMMARY
(Erase heading not required.)

Army Form C. 2118

Instructions regarding War Diaries and Intelligence Summaries are contained in F. S. Regs., Part II. and the Staff Manual respectively. Title Pages will be prepared in manuscript.

Place	Date	Hour	Summary of Events and Information	Remarks and references to Appendices
BAILLEUVAL LENS II	27		Refilled from lorries and delivered. Weather cold & dull	E.J.
	28		Coy marched to SAULTY at 10 am refilled from lorries and delivered. Weather dull	E.J.
SAULTY	29		Refilled from lorries by marched at noon to N of AUTHIE delivered. Weather dull	E.J.
AUTHIE	30		Refilled at 9.30 am and delivered. T.1/09492 at BRIDSON RD evacuated 2 M unit to C.C.S and struck off. Weather wet	E.J.
	31		Refill at 9.30 am and delivered. Weather fine.	E.J.

E. Taff Capt
O.C. No 2 Company
H 21st Divisional Train

No 2 Coy
1/1st Divisional Train B.E.F. France

WAR DIARY
or
INTELLIGENCE SUMMARY

Army Form C. 2118

Place	Date	Hour	Summary of Events and Information	Remarks and references to Appendices
AUTHIE LENS 11	1	April	Refilled from Lorries at 8 a.m and delivered to units by 10 a.m. Lorries left area at 5.30 p.m to MARIEUX and delivered to Coy units in new area. Recruit refill from Lorries for delivery 2nd inst at 6.30 p.m. T5/8951 A/Cpl JOBSON T.E. promoted Lance Cpl. 149/12,291 Pte STEWART A.C. evacuation to No 3 Italy hospital sick struck off the strength. Weather stormy	C.J.
MARIEUX	2	"	Coy marched at 1.30 p.m to ORVILLE and delivered supplies in new area. Refilled from Lorries and supply wagons from units for mail journey. Weather dull	C.J.
ORVILLE	3	"	Coy H.Q. marched with Bde transport at 9.0 a.m to HH PETIT HOUVIN DOULLENS and FREVENT and entrained at 7 p.m. Weather dull	C.J.
noh HAZEBROU -CK 5A	4	"	Coy H.Q. detrained at PESELHOEK (BELGIUM) at 5 a.m and marched to POPERINGHE. Lalr H.MORRIS A.S.C and 5 O.R returned from leave. Supply wagons reported from units. Coy marched at 3 p.m to BALL CAMP Sheet 27 L 3, 6 5.6 refilled from Lorries and delivered. Weather damp	C.J.
sheet 27 L3.6.56	5	"	Refilled from Lorries at 9 a.m and delivered. Weather damp	C.J.
"	6	"	Routine as usual 13/07805 1/Cpl PARKER R.W. reduced to permanent grade of driver (drunk). Weather wet	C.J.

WAR DIARY
or
INTELLIGENCE SUMMARY

(Erase heading not required.)

Army Form C. 2118

Instructions regarding War Diaries and Intelligence Summaries are contained in F. S. Regs., Part II. and the Staff Manual respectively. Title Pages will be prepared in manuscript.

Place	Date	Hour	Summary of Events and Information	Remarks and references to Appendices
Sheet 27 23 b 5.6	7 April 1918		Refill as usual by HQ marched at 10.30am to VLAMERTINGHE Shed 28 H.14 A.6.4. Weather still	G.S.
Sheet 28 H.14 a.6.4	8	—	Refill from Lorries and delivered. Lorries bulk from Lorries to refill got. Weather still	G.S.
	9	"	Sent in bulk from VLAMERTINGHE Railhead with horse transport. Refill as per supplies drawn 8th and delivered. T/35269 Pte SKELDON S. admitted to 138 Field Ambulance. Weather still	G.S.
	10		Sent in bulk from Railhead refilled and delivered by HQ marched at 10.30am to POPERINGHE Sheet 28 G.4 a. 3.0 Weather stormy	G.S.
Sheet 28 G.4.a.3.0.	11	—	Refilled from Lorries and delivered T/302623 Dr McNEE. D. admitted to 10/139. Field Ambulance. Weather still	G.S.
	12	—	Refilled at 1.30pm Baggage wagons returned from units. The following personnel and transport having become surplus to establishment posted by the strength from 9th inst. T/331107 Dr FANCOURT H.M. T/248399 Dr WYATT L. 4 HD horses and 2 G.S. wagons. N T4/243101 Dr NEWEY H. 2 HD horses and 1 G.S. wagon transferred to No.1 Coy train from and being to formation of the Div M.G. Batt. T/35626 Y Pte SKELDON S. evacuated to 64 C.C.S. and struck off the strength. Weather stormy	G.S.
	13		Refilled at 2.30pm 3 O.R returned from leave weather still	G.S.

WAR DIARY
or
INTELLIGENCE SUMMARY
(Erase heading not required.)

Army Form C. 2118

Place	Date	Hour	Summary of Events and Information	Remarks and references to Appendices
Hou 2 & G 4 & 3.0.	14 April		Refill from Lozins at 2.30 p.m. and delivered. Weather dull	
	15		Routine as usual. Baggage wagons sent to units. Weather dull	
	16		Routine as usual. 73/026231 Pte McNEE D. evacuated to CCS on 13th inst and since tft. Weather dull	
	17		Tractor proceeded at 6.30 am to PESELHOEK Railhead and left about 8am owing to following casualties. Killed 12521 Sgt SELBY E.C. 201301 Pte CLARK J.P. } attached from 238 Employment Company 74/094206 Dr CROCKER S.J. attached Lambs I boy train 5 HD Horses 1 Riden 1 G.S. wagon destroyed. Wounded 54/042242 Rfle BARON W. } admitted to 189 Field Ambulance 13/027003 Dr MURRAY M. 7/39205 Pte MITTEN J. attached from 1 boy train } admitted to 27 Field Ambulance 201630 Pte DAVIES E. attached from 238 Employ Coy 4 HD horses sent to PROVEN Railhead refilled from Lozres at 5 pm and delivered. S2/016374 Pte BATCHELOR G. admitted to 139 FA. Weather dull	

WAR DIARY
or
INTELLIGENCE SUMMARY
(Erase heading not required.)

Army Form C. 2118

Instructions regarding War Diaries and Intelligence Summaries are contained in F.S. Regs, Part II. and the Staff Manual respectively. Title Pages will be prepared in manuscript.

Place	Date	Hour	Summary of Events and Information	Remarks and references to Appendices
Thiel 28 G 4 R 30	18 April		Seen in truth from PROVEN Marthes by horse transport utilised in transit at 2.30 pm and delivered. T3/024039 Sgt ROBERTSON.W.P. admitted to 13.9 F.A. TM/10824Y Dr BURGESS.J admitted to hospital while on leave in England and struck off strength from 24th of March. 2HD 1 Riek and 41 D humanely attacked from No1 Coy of train destroyed by Shell fire 19th and struck off strength still	C.S.
	19		Notified from Lorries at 1.45 pm and delivered. 3HD evacuated and 16 SAA wagon destroyed by shell fire 19th struck off strength still Burnt lorries on B line Tanks held at 6.0 p.m. Burnt at Thiel 28 A22 b-45. New G Plot 2.	C.S.
	20	"	Routine as usual S4/042242 b/k BARON.W and T3/024003 MURRAY.M evacuated to 36 c.C.S 19th and struck off Weather fine	C.S.
	21	"	Routine as usual T3/024039 Sgt ROBERTSON.W.P and S2/018394 Pte BATCHELOR.G evacuated to C.C.S 19th and struck off Weather fine	C.S.
	22	"	Routine as usual Baggage wagons reported from unit Weather fine	C.S.
	23	"	Routine as usual Weather fine	C.S.
	24	"	Routine as usual Weather still	C.S.
	25	-	Routine as usual Baggage wagons sent to units Weather fine	C.S.

WAR DIARY
or
INTELLIGENCE SUMMARY

(Erase heading not required.)

Army Form C. 2118

Place	Date	Hour	Summary of Events and Information	Remarks and references to Appendices
Sheet 28 G4A 3.0	26 April		Remained as usual. 1 coy marched at 8.12 am to POPERINGHE — WOESTEN Road Sheet 28. A16.a.9.5 Weather dull	N.S.
Sheet 28 A16.a.9.5	27	—	Rifleman Camp at 12.30 pm from Lorries and arrived coy marched at 2.30 pm to POPERINGHE – PROVEN Road Sheet 27 F28.c.8.4 Weather damp	N.S.
Sheet 27 F28.c.8.4	28	—	Coy in Bivth from PROVEN Railroad at 9.45 a.m by horse transport. Rifles in camp and delivered. 9 H.D. + 1 Motor received from Miniouris and taken in the strength. SN/60466 L/Cpl ROSSER J.L. and T4/060677 Dr BENTLEY J.T. joined from Base depot and taken on the strength. T/304906 Dr BRADBURY W.T. and T/341843 Dr BUTLER C.H. joined from Base depot posted to No 1 Coy. Train to coy and permanently attached to this coy. Weather dull	
	29	"	Horse transport proceeded to PROVEN Railroad to draw in bulk at 8.45 am. Railroad shelled after half rations had been drawn. The following casualties were caused — 2 Lt S.G. ALDOUS S.C. wounded and admitted to T4/094166 Dr PARKS.G. No 1 Coy train 223973 Pte POULTER.G. 2015to O'DONNELL.E. 238 Empty coy field ambulance 2 H.D. horses No 1 coy killed. 1 H.D. horse wounded since destroyed. 1 G.S. wagon No 1 coy train destroyed by fire at Railhead	

WAR DIARY or INTELLIGENCE SUMMARY

Army Form C. 2118

(Erase heading not required.)

Instructions regarding War Diaries and Intelligence Summaries are contained in F.S. Regs., Part II. and the Staff Manual respectively. Title Pages will be prepared in manuscript.

Place	Date	Hour	Summary of Events and Information	Remarks and references to Appendices
Sheet 28 G 4 a 30	18 April		Saw in truth from PREVEN Northward by horse transport rifled in camp at 2.30 pm and delivered. T3/024039 Sgt ROBERTSON. W.P. admitted to 13.9 F.A. 14/08244 Dr BURGESS. T admitted to hospital whilst on leave in England and struck off the strength from 24th of March. 2 H.D. 1 Riding and 4 H.D. heavily attacked from 1 to 1 box of train destroyed by rail fire 19th and struck off. Weather still	C.J.
	19	"	Rifled from Lorries at 1.45 pm and delivered. 3 H D arrived and 1 G.S. wagon destroyed by rail fire 19th struck off. Weather still. Burial Service on 3 other ranks held at 6.0 pm. Buried at Sheet 28 A 22 b 4.5 Row G Plot 2.	C.J.
	20	"	Routine as usual. S4/042242 Lft BARON. W. and T3/024003 Dr MURRAY. M. evacuated to 36 C.C.S. 19th and struck off. Weather fine	C.J.
	21	"	Routine as usual. T3/024039 Sgt ROBERTSON. W.P. and S2/018394 Pte BATCHELOR. G. evacuated to C.C.S. 18th and struck off. Weather fine	C.J.
	22	"	Routine as usual. Baggage wagons returned from under Heavy fire	C.J.
	23	"	Routine as usual. Weather fine	C.J.
	24	"	Routine as usual. Weather still	C.J.
	25	-	Routine as usual. Baggage wagons sent to units. Weather fine	C.J.

WAR DIARY
or
INTELLIGENCE SUMMARY
(Erase heading not required.)

Army Form C. 2118

Instructions regarding War Diaries and Intelligence Summaries are contained in F.S. Regs., Part II. and the Staff Manual respectively. Title Pages will be prepared in manuscript.

Place	Date	Hour	Summary of Events and Information	Remarks and references to Appendices
Sheet 27 G.14.a.3.0.	26 April		Routine as usual. Coy marched at 8.12 pm to POPERINGHE — WOESTEN Road Sheet 28.A.16.a.9.5. Weather dull	W.J.
Sheet 28 A.16.a.9.5	27	—	Rifleman camp at 12.30 pm Lorries arrived Coy marched out 2.30 pm to POPERINGHE — PROVEN Road Sheet 27 F.29.c.8.4. Weather damp	W.J.
Sheet 27 F.29.c.8.4	28	—	Coy in Butts from PROVEN Road Railhead at 9.45am by horse transport. Rifles in camp and delivered. 9 H.D. + 9 Mules received from Remounts and taken in the strength. 54/60466 L/Cpl ROSSER. J.L. and T4/060677 Dr BENTLEY. J.T. joined from Base depot and taken on the strength. T/304906 Dr BRADBURY W.T. and T/341843 Dr BUTLER C.H. joined from Base depot posts to No 1 Coy Train L.J. and permanently attached to this Coy. Weather dull	L.J.
	29	"	Horse transport proceeded to PROVEN Railhead to draw in full at 8.45am Railhead shelled after motors had been drawn. The following casualties were caused — 2 Lt S.G. ALDOUS S.C. T4/094166 Dr PARKS.G. No.1 Coy Train 2235913 Pte POULTER.G. 201500 " O'DONNELL.E. 238 Supy Coy / wounded and admitted to Field Ambulance / 2 H.D. horses No.1 Coy Killed. 1 H.D. horse wounded since destroyed. 1 G.S. wagon No.1 Coy Train destroyed by fire at Railhead	

WAR DIARY
INTELLIGENCE SUMMARY

Army Form C. 2118

Place	Date	Hour	Summary of Events and Information	Remarks and references to Appendices
Nutley FSG E&H 23.4	29		Remainder of suffered trench system between 8.30 p.m. & 3.30 p.m. expecting an enemy counter attack at 13.02 & 14.2 at MACINTYRE D and 1/3 & 1/2 & at WALSH. Enemy forces from the north of their day and intercepted at 13.58 with purpose. Enemy counter attack by enemy 2nd Forces M1.47 and 1st Division at 15.47 at MACINTYRE Bay. Enemy fire was abandoned off north Beating.	C.J.
	30		Some heavy patrons book by our troops from between Nutley and Glenroy. Replied such enemy our about following way. Weather cool.	C.J.

Signed K. Wright Rooke
Lt. 2 Roy
1/1/1.26 Liverpool Regt.

No 2 Company A.S.C.
1st Twickenham   FRANCE   MAY 1918

Army Form C. 2118.

WAR DIARY
or
INTELLIGENCE SUMMARY
(Erase heading not required.)

Instructions regarding War Diaries and Intelligence Summaries are contained in F.S. Regs, Part II. and the Staff Manual respectively. Title pages will be prepared in manuscript.

Place	Date	Hour	Summary of Events and Information	Remarks and references to Appendices
Sht 27 F28 C8 4	1	May	Driver Ruffles Walker 30th Killed from Enemy Aeroplane shell gotshell hit lorry mat lot at 1.30 p.m. 6 W of POPERING HE-PROVEN road Sht 27 F29.a.65. Weather dull	C.I.
Sht 27 B27 a.6.5	2	—	Routine as usual weather fine	C.I.
	3	—	Routine as usual. Baggage wagon aprives from units TM/094168 Pte PARKES A. attached from No 1 Coy & 201830 Pte DAVIES E. attached from 238 Emp Coy commanded advances to C.S. amateur in off Weather very fine	C.I.
	4	—	Routine as usual H.O. Rif juious from 238 Employment Coy. Weather fine	C.I.
	5	—	Routine as usual 223893 Pte POULTER E & 201500 Pte O'DONNELL E. remained & returnes to attual oft. 2 O.R. proceed from 238 Emp Coy where Satupy a London TM/046218 W HURST R.J. extension of 1/14th with pay TM/235534 Cpl A. CHIDGEY. & transferred from No 3 Coy Walkania	C.I.
	6	—	8 pairs + wagon sent to ROUSBRUGGE Railway to anaure Bath to drive lorries TM/11655 Sgt COVEY G, S4/035698 L/Cpl WINKLEY A E T/389419 Pte HUMPHRIES G, T/294419, Pte TAYLOR J, much for Bean What now taken on the strength 1 N.C.O posted from Emp Coy S4/060464 S/Sgt ROSSER J.O transferred to No 3 Coy, M32/016383 Pte COWLING W. transferred from No 4 Coy Weather fine	C.I.

Army Form C. 2118.

WAR DIARY
or
INTELLIGENCE SUMMARY.
(Erase heading not required.)

Instructions regarding War Diaries and Intelligence Summaries are contained in F. S. Regs., Part II. and the Staff Manual respectively. Title pages will be prepared in manuscript.

Place	Date	Hour	Summary of Events and Information	Remarks and references to Appendices
Port of Arr. P.S.A. 56	May 7		Routine as usual weather wet	C.V.
	8		Routine as usual weather fine	C.V.
	9		Routine as usual Weather fine	C.V.
	10		Routine as usual Weather fine	C.V.
	11		Routine as usual T4/249518 Pte HOPPER.J.R. T3/024826 Pte HUGHES W. T4/041410 Pte WICKENDEN F. joining from Base Depot and taken on the strength. T4/083268 Pte PEATTIE T. transfrd to 1221st Bde H.Q. and struck off. Weather fine	C.J.
	12		Routine as usual weather damp	C.J.
	13		Routine as usual T4/065206 Pte GEORGE.H. T3/024826 Pte HUGHES.W. and T/294419 Pte TAYLOR J. transferred to 158 Field Ambulance and struck off. Weather wet.	C.J.
	14		Routine as usual 2nd Lieut S.G.ALDOUS. A.S.C. evacuated to England onwards 4th May and struck off. weather fine	C.J.
	15		Routine as usual weather fine	C.J.

A 5834 Wt. W 4973/M637 750,000 8/16 D. D. & L. Ltd. Forms/C2118/13

WAR DIARY
or
INTELLIGENCE SUMMARY.
(Erase heading not required.)

Army Form C. 2118.

Place	Date	Hour	Summary of Events and Information	Remarks and references to Appendices
Sheet 27 F.27.a.5.5	16 May		Routine as usual Tw/124 953 Wheeler G/Pl WALKER S.G. admitted to 139 F.A. TW/198191 A/2/14 JONES. S.G. promoted L/Cpl. as from 2.2.15. Weather fine.	G.J.
	17		Routine as usual 1HD received from remounts. Weather fine.	G.J.
	18		Routine as usual. 2nd Lieut. P.R.L. SAVILL. A.S.C having been former entrl for general service for a period of three months his attach off me L.J. strength from 3rd inst. Weather fine.	G.J.
	19		Routine as usual Weather fine	G.J.
	20		Routine as usual. Weather fine	G.J.
	21		Routine as usual. Weather fine	G.J.
	22		Routine as usual 2nd Lieut. W.F. PICKFORD. A.S.C. joy from 21st inst. Weather fine.	G.J.
	23		Routine as usual Weather fine	G.J.
	24		Routine as usual 2/Lt. A.W.RUSTON. A.S.C. posted to this weather fine unit from 14th Brunel	G.J.
	25		Routine as usual Weather fine.	G.J.

WAR DIARY
or
INTELLIGENCE SUMMARY.
(Erase heading not required.)

Army Form C. 2118.

Place	Date	Hour	Summary of Events and Information	Remarks and references to Appendices
Beek 27 F2/A.55	26 May		Routine as usual. Weather fine	E.?
	27		Routine as usual. No 7/356239 Pte WILLIAMS. C.W joined from Base Depot and taken on the strength. Weather fine	E.?
	28		Routine as usual. No 405580 Pte WATSON. J. 239 Empty bogy rejoined from labour corps 130pm depot. Weather fine	E.?
	29		Routine as usual. Weather fine	E.?
	30		Routine as usual. The following casualties were caused at 9.30 pm on 29th inst by a shell bursting in a small tank.	E.?
			No T/4/081133 C.Q.M.S BARRETT. P.W.F. } killed	
			" T/3/022984 Sgt BULL. W. }	
			" S/4/890116 Sgt NAISMITH. A.N. }	
			" SS/1704 Sgt MONTEATH. W.B. } sick of wounds	
			" T/4/198191 L/Cpl JONES. S.G. }	
			" T/4/195434 Dvr L/Cpl LUGG. J.H. }	
			" T/4/294519 Dvr HOPPER. J.R. } killed	
			" T/35519 Dvr PERKINS. F.W. }	
			" 201540 Pte DAVENPORT. T. 238 Empty bogy attached wounded	
	31		Routine as usual. Weather fine	E.?

CAPTAIN,
O.C. No. 2 COY, 41st DIVISIONAL TRAIN

No 2 Company
H ol Div Train

Army Form C. 2118.

WAR DIARY
or
INTELLIGENCE SUMMARY
(Erase heading not required.)

JUNE 1918.

Place	Date	Hour	Summary of Events and Information	Remarks and references to Appendices
Gula Sheet 27 F.27.a.5.5.	1st June		Supply Wagon moved off at 8 am & drew from Railhead 3 ual lorries & 1 ult GS Wagon 9.30 am. Refill 1.30 pm. T/13119 T.SSM. Eycott F. Mentioned in despatches. Weather fine	C.J.
"	2nd		Routine as usual. Baggage Wagon joined Units. 1 BA. Emby ASC returned from course of Anti Gas School. Weather fine	C.J.
"	3rd		Supply Wagon delivered Ration 8.45 am. to ZEGGER CAPPEL Area arriving about 3 pm. Refill fine transport at 6 pm from lorries at 6 pm Weather fine	C.J.
ZEGGER CAPPEL	4th		All transport 122 Inf Bde. moved 6.40 am. under OC No 2 Coy. to EPERLECQUES Area. Coy arrived destination BLEUE MAISON at 11 am. Supply Wagon delivered Rations in new Area. Refill from lorries at 3 pm. WEATHER fine	C.J.
Bleue Maison	5th		Supply Wagon delivered rations at 10 am. Refill at 1 pm. " fine	
"	6th		Routine as usual. Baggage Wagons rejoined from Units. The following R.C.O.'s joined from A.S.C. Base @ Depot. T/215859 CQMS Johnston L.A. T/237491 Sergt. Scott J.E. Weather fine	C.J.
	7th		Routine as usual. The following R.C.O's joined from ASC Base Depot. S/1146290 Sergt Goodman A. S/090712 Sergt Stewart A. Div Supply Wagon, Signal & RE Linders joined company for duty. Weather fine	C.J.

WAR DIARY
INTELLIGENCE SUMMARY.

(Erase heading not required.)

Army Form C. 2118.

Place	Date	Hour	Summary of Events and Information	Remarks and references to Appendices
Bleu Maison	8		Ration drawn from Railhead at 10.0 a.m by Horse Transport. No refill. 2 Baggage Wagon joined from Div. H.Q.	Weather fine. R.J.
"	9		Ration drawn from Railhead at 10.0 a.m by Horse Transport. Refilled at 11.0 AM Recruit 7/39285 Dr Fleming. I. joined from Base Depot.	Weather fine R.J.
"	10		Routine as usual.	Weather cloudy & showery R.J.
"	11		Ration drawn from Railhead at 9.30 AM by Horse Transport. Refilled at 11.0 AM	Weather fine R.J.
"	12		Routine as usual	Weather fine R.J.
"	13		Routine as usual. 2 Baggage Wagon returned from 19th Mx Pioneers.	Weather fine R.J.
"	14		Routine as usual	Weather fine R.J.
"	15		Routine as usual	Weather fine R.J.
"	16		Routine as usual. Joined from ASC Base Depot - T/198381 Dr. REDSHAW J.E.	Weather fine R.J.
"	17		Routine as usual	Weather fine R.J.
"	18		Routine as usual	Weather fine R.J.

Army Form C. 2118.

WAR DIARY
or
INTELLIGENCE SUMMARY.
(Erase heading not required.)

Instructions regarding War Diaries and Intelligence Summaries are contained in F. S. Regs., Part II. and the Staff Manual respectively. Title pages will be prepared in manuscript.

Place	Date	Hour	Summary of Events and Information	Remarks and references to Appendices
27 NE AND 27 SE Lig C 2.6	19-6-18		Routine as usual. C.O. inspected 1st line of Transport. Weather wet	le.1.
"	20-6-18		Routine as usual. Weather fine during day showery at night	le.1.
"	21-6-18		Routine as usual. 234119 Dr Hilton transferred to 122 Inf B.H.Q. Weather fine	le.1.
"	22-6-18		Routine as usual. Weather fine	le.1.
"	23-6-18		Routine as usual. Weather fine	le.1.
"	24-6-18		Routine as usual. Baggage Waggon left for Maili. Weather fine	le.1.
SHEET 27 NE J 22 d 3.4	25-6-18		Company left Bleue Maison at 9.0 A.M. Arrived (SHEET 27) H.11. A.8.2 2.0 P.M. Refilled at Bleue Maison at 11.30 A.M. Weather fine	le.1.
"	26-6-18		Supply Wagon moved at 9.0 A.M. Company moved at 11.45 A.M. arrived Le Temple (LE TEMPLE) 3.30 P.M. Refilled at 1.30 P.M. Weather fine	le.1.
"	27-6-18		Supply Col brought rations. refilled at 2-0 P.M. Weather fine	le.1.
"	28-6-18		Supply Col brought rations refilled at 2-0 P.M. Weather fine	le.1.
"	29-6-18		Ration Wagon from Railhead 12-30 A.M. Refilled 1-30 Weather fine	le.1.

WAR DIARY
INTELLIGENCE SUMMARY.
(Erase heading not required.)

Army Form C. 2118.

Place	Date	Hour	Summary of Events and Information	Remarks and references to Appendices
SHEET 27 J 21 d 3.4.	25/9/16		Ration drawn from Railhead. Refilled at 2.45 and again at 6 pm	C.2.

Army Form C. 2118.

WAR DIARY
or
INTELLIGENCE SUMMARY.
(Erase heading not required.)

Instructions regarding War Diaries and Intelligence Summaries are contained in F. S. Regs., Part II. and the Staff Manual respectively. Title pages will be prepared in manuscript.

Place	Date	Hour	Summary of Events and Information	Remarks and references to Appendices
MAP REF. SHEET 27 K.26 c.4.8	1-7-18		Company moved from Le Temple [LE TEMPLE] at 8.30 A.M. Arrived at STEENVOORDE at 9.15 A.M. Supply Wagon left for Unit at 5:0 A.M. Refilled at 11:30 P.M. Weather fine	L.J.
"	2-7-18		Routine as usual. Refilled at 1.45 p.m. ditto	L.J.
MAP REF SHEET 27 K.27 a.3.10	3-7-18		Routine as usual. Refilled at 11.0 A.M. ditto	L.J.
"	4-7-18		Routine as usual. Refilled at 2.0 p.m. ditto	L.J.
"	5-7-18		Routine as usual. Joined from BHTD (T/38#8#0 Dr. Cox J (T/262336 " Cox G.W. Refilled at 2.0 p.m. ditto	L.J.
"	6-7-18		T/240.21 Corpl. FINBOW B.J. died in 36 C.C.S. and struck off. Routine as usual. Div Commander inspected the Company Refilled at 2.0 p.m. ditto	L.J.
"	7-7-18		Routine as usual. Capt C TRIPP went on leave to England. 2nd Lt. W F PICKFORD assumed Command. ditto	L.J.
"	8-7-18		Routine as usual	L.J.
"	9-7-18		Routine as usual. Company was inspected, mounted, 2.30 p.m. by Lt Col. T. DOWLING Fine	L.J.

Army Form C. 2118.

WAR DIARY
INTELLIGENCE SUMMARY.
(Erase heading not required.)

Instructions regarding War Diaries and Intelligence Summaries are contained in F. S. Regs., Part II. and the Staff Manual respectively. Title pages will be prepared in manuscript.

Place	Date	Hour	Summary of Events and Information	Remarks and references to Appendices
"	10.7.18		Routine as usual Weather wet & heavy afternoon storm	Ap. 1
"	11.7.18		Routine as usual Weather wet	Ap. 1
"	12.7.18		Routine as usual T4 235281 Driver Wilson J E) proceeded to England on leave 403580 Private Watson J) Weather wet	Ap. 1
"	13.7.18		Routine as usual Weather fine	Ap. 1
"	14.7.18		Routine as usual TS 7776 Dvr WR Phillips. S proceeded to England on leave. Weather fine	Ap. 1
"	15.7.18		Routine as usual weather wet	Ap. 1
"	16.7.18		Routine as usual weather showery	Ap. 1
"	17.7.18		Routine as usual Baggage Wagon left at 6.30 pm for Minik weather fine	Ap. 1
H.26.d.7.5	18.7.18		Routine as usual Company moved to new farm during morning weather fine	Ap. 1
"	19.7.18		Routine as usual weather fine	Ap. 1
"	20.7.18		Routine as usual Pte Corfe W leave to England Rain & thunderstorm	Ap. 1
"	21.7.18		Routine as usual weather fine	Ap. 1

Army Form C. 2118.

WAR DIARY
or
INTELLIGENCE SUMMARY.

(Erase heading not required.)

Instructions regarding War Diaries and Intelligence Summaries are contained in F. S. Regs., Part II. and the Staff Manual respectively. Title pages will be prepared in manuscript.

Place	Date	Hour	Summary of Events and Information	Remarks and references to Appendices
R26 d. 7. 9.	22.7.18		Routine as usual. Weather fine	le.?
"	23.7.18		Routine as usual. Weather very wet	le.?
"	24.7.18		Routine as usual. Dr Ball E. Leave to England. Weather fair to wet	le.?
"	25.7.18		Routine as usual. Weather fine	le.?
"	26.7.18		Routine as usual. Weather showery	le.?
"	27.7.18		Routine as usual. " wet	le.?
"	28.7.18		Routine as usual. " cloudy & dull	le.?
"	29.7.18		Routine as usual. " fine	le.?
"	30.7.18		Routine as usual TH/27501s Dr Newbold F. transferred to 138th Field Amb " very fine	le.?
"	31.7.18		Routine as usual. Baggage Wagons reporent from Units " very fine	le.?

_____ CAPTAIN,
O.C. No. 2 COY. 41st DIVISIONAL TRAIN

Army Form C. 2118.

WAR DIARY
or
INTELLIGENCE SUMMARY.
(Erase heading not required.)

Instructions regarding War Diaries and Intelligence Summaries are contained in F. S. Regs., Part II. and the Staff Manual respectively. Title pages will be prepared in manuscript.

Place	Date	Hour	Summary of Events and Information	Remarks and references to Appendices
27 K 26 d 7 9	1.8.18		Routine as usual. Iran to milk 8.45 a.m. Drawn from Railhead 10.30 a.m. Refill at 2.10 p.m. 15th Hants Baggage Supply Wagon left. Own with Unit. 201476 Pte ASHCROFT R. proceeded on leave to England. Weather very fine	16.8
"	2.8.18		T 261678 Pte BLUNDELL F } proceeded on leave to 201559 " ANDERSON C. } England. Weather very wet.	16.8
"	3.8.18		Routine as usual. Weather showery	16.8
"	4.8.18		Routine as usual. 2nd Lt ROULSTON A.W. went on 4 days course XIX Corps School. Weather fine	16.8
"	5.8.18		Routine as usual. DHQ Baggage Wagon returned. Weather cloudy, rain in evening	16.8
"	6.8.18		Routine as usual. " " stormy	16.8
"	7.8.18		Routine as usual. " " fine + sunny	16.8
"	8.8.18		Routine as usual. 15th Bratt Hants Baggage Wagon returned. fine intervals of rain	16.8
"	9.8.18		Routine as usual. 15th Bratt Hants Baggage Wagon left for Unit. T4/057287 Dr Miller J proceeded on leave to U.K. fine T 370444 Pte Payne W T4/56635 " Petty E } Joined from BHTP T4/047250 " Paul J.W. } Leather making T4/259485 " Parker J.	16.8
"	10.8.18		Routine as usual " " 8 very fine + sunny	16.8

WAR DIARY
or
INTELLIGENCE SUMMARY.
(Erase heading not required.)

Army Form C. 2118.

Place	Date	Hour	Summary of Events and Information	Remarks and references to Appendices
27 K2d 7.9	11.8.18		2/Lt ROWLSTON A W returned from Gas Course	
			Routine as usual	Weather very fine
"	12.8.18		Dr STOKES D W leave to England T3.028355	"
			The following left for the 13HTD to train Hunt Baggage wagon returned	
			{ Dr MATHEWS J T3.067087	
			Dr OVERTON C T.372.15	
			Dr POOLES R T T/7062479	
			Dr TAYLOR H T/7094247	
			Br WICKHAM F T/7041418 }	
"	13.8.18		Routine as usual	"
"	14.8.18		Routine as usual	"
"	15.8.18		Routine as usual 2nd Lt W F PICKFORD proceeded on leave to UK	"
"	16.8.18		Routine as usual	"
"	17.8.18		Routine as usual T/4.065218 L/Cpl HURST R J proceeded on leave to UK	Weather fine
			109272 PTE DEA H	
"	18.8.18		Routine as usual T.20336 Fr S Sergt PULLEN H proceeded on leave to UK	"
"	19.8.18		Routine as usual	very fine
"	20.8.18		Drew from railhead 10.15 Refilled at 2.0 p.m.	"
"	21.8.18		Routine as usual	"
"	22.8.18		Routine as usual Capt MORRIS H proceeded on leave to UK	" hot
"	23.8.18		Routine as usual	fine
"	24.8.18		Routine as usual	"
"	25.8.18		Routine as usual T/894417 Dr NELSON S B admitted to 13DRS Field Amb S/294998 PTE PRESTON M to 13HT Depot	"
"	26.8.18		Routine as usual	rain in evening

Army Form C. 2118.

WAR DIARY
or
INTELLIGENCE SUMMARY
(Erase heading not required.)

Place	Date	Hour	Summary of Events and Information	Remarks and references to Appendices
27K26&7 9	27.8.18		Routine as usual. 158162 Pte CPL SHARP went on leave to U.K. Weather fine Thunderstorm evening	L.T
	28.8.18		Return drawn from Railhead in trucks. Company moved at 12 noon for RENESCURE arrived RENESCURE 6.0 p.m. T/H 4057365 Dr EDINBOROUGH I.R.R. proceeded on leave to the U.K. Weather very hot, heavy storms/rain	L.T
RENESCURE	29.8.18		Company left RENESCURE by Road at 8.0 a.m. for HALLINES arrived HALLINES 11.45 a.m. Refilled at 1.30 and again at 5.30 p.m. from lorries	L.T
HALLINES	30.8.18		Routine as usual Weather fine & sunny	L.T
	31.8.18		Routine as usual. Reinforcement 52/016383 Pte COWLING W. report to United Kingdom. Weather fine. Delivered rations and straw from LUMBRES by M.T. at 9 am refilled at 11.15am	L.T

[signature]
CAPTAIN
O.C. No. 7 COY. 41ST DIVISIONAL TRAIN

Army Form C. 2118.

WAR DIARY
or
INTELLIGENCE SUMMARY.
(Erase heading not required.)

Instructions regarding War Diaries and Intelligence Summaries are contained in F. S. Regs., Part II. and the Staff Manual respectively. Title pages will be prepared in manuscript.

Place	Date	Hour	Summary of Events and Information	Remarks and references to Appendices
HALLINES	1.9.18		Company left by road for Calais Aerodrome at 7.0 A.M. arrived at 5.0 p.m. Refilled from Motor Lorries at 5.10 p.m. T/058569 Dr ALLDER A.E. proceeded on leave to the United Kingdom	L.T.
	2.9.18		Refilled at 3.0 p.m. from Motor Lorries. Weather fine	L.T.
ABEELE				
M.18.c.7.9	3.9.18		Company moved at 1.0 p.m to } RAILHEAD arrived 2.0 p.m }	L.T.
	4.9.18		" " " "	L.T.
	5.9.18		Rations drawn from Railhead by 14 T at 11.15 A.M	L.T.
	6.9.18		T5/8393 Fr Cpl TASKER W. proceeded on leave to the U.K. Routine as per the 5th sunny	L.T.
27/6.28 L.2.H	7.9.18		Company left by road for WIPPENHOEK RAILHEAD at 8.30 A.M. arrived 10.15 A.M. weather fine	L.T.
			Supply Wagon left for WIPPENHOEK RAILHEAD at 6.20 A.M. Refilled at 2.0 p.m. showery with thunder	
	8.9.18		Rations delivered from Railhead at 8.30 A.M.	
			Rations delivered to Units at 7.0 A.M. WEATHER Very wet—heavy rain	L.T.
			by H.T. Refilled at 10.30 A.M.	
	9.9.18		Routine as usual " showery + windy	L.T.
	10.9.18		" " fine	L.T.
	11.9.18		Rations delivered at 8.15 A.M. Rations drawn from Railhead 10.45 A.M. Refilled	L.T.

WAR DIARY
or
INTELLIGENCE SUMMARY.

(Erase heading not required.)

Army Form C. 2118.

Place	Date	Hour	Summary of Events and Information	Remarks and references to Appendices
27628 624	11.9.18	11.30 A.M	T3/027805 Dr PARKER. W Proceeded on leave to the U.K. Weather wet + windy	L.T
"	12.9.18		Routine as usual. Weather very wet with electrical storm	L.T
"	13.9.18		T/4820 Dr MEAGHER. P Proceeded on leave to U.K. Baggage wagon to Unit for day only	L.T
"	14.9.18		" " "	L.T
"	15.9.18	7.6 A.M	Rations delivered at 7.6 A.M refilled at 10.45 A.M Weather very fine	L.T
"	16.9.18		Routine as above " " "	L.T
"	17.9.18		Routine as usual. Heavy thunder storm in the early morning Very fine during day	L.T
"	18.9.18		340/079797 Pte BRADBURY. H Gone to U.K. Weather fine	L.T
"	19.9.18		" " "	L.T
"	20.9.18	8.30 A.M	Rations delivered to unit at 8.30 A.M Baggage wagon drew from Railhead – Conveyed ration to MT Col. STEENVOORDE (STEEN VOORDE) T304906 Dr BRADBURY W.T T/4820 Dr YARDLEY F.J Proceeded on leave to the T307635 Dr YARDLEY F.J United Kingdom 352249 Pte QUARRY. T Weather fine	L.T

Army Form C. 2118.

WAR DIARY
or
INTELLIGENCE SUMMARY.
(Erase heading not required.)

Instructions regarding War Diaries and Intelligence Summaries are contained in F.S. Regs., Part II. and the Staff Manual respectively. Title pages will be prepared in manuscript.

Place	Date	Hour	Summary of Events and Information	Remarks and references to Appendices
27/L28 & 24	21.9.18		Routine as usual	
	22.9.18		" " Weather windy & showery	
	23.9.18		" " Weather fine	
	24.9.18		207793 Pte DISLEY L proceeded on leave to U.K.	
	25.9.18		7406857S Cpl BOLTON JJ	
	26.9.18		Baggage wagon sent to Unit	
	27.9.18		Ration drawn from railhead at 10.30 and delivered at 13.30. Attacked Supply	L.T.
			Wagon DHQ, Signal, CRE, M.G.13, MVS joined Div troops Nº2 Group on the Weather fine	
28/9 11 A 20	28.9.18		afternoon. Routine as for 27th. Company moved at 18.00 o'clock for Ridge (RIDGE	
		19.55	CAMP) arrived 19.55. Weather wet in the morning cleared & fine for remainder of day	
	29.9.18		Rations arrived by Supply Col motor at 8.15. Refilled and delivered	
			rations to Units. 154515 Pte CATON proceeded on leave to United	
			Kingdom. Weather fine morning. Rain set in during afternoon	
	30.9.18		Rations as for 29th. 158592 Pte WILSON CA proceeded on leave 15 U.K. Weather wet	

WAR DIARY
or
INTELLIGENCE SUMMARY.
(Erase heading not required.)

Army Form C. 2118.

Place	Date	Hour	Summary of Events and Information	Remarks and references to Appendices
28/G 11 a.o.o.	1.10.18		Rations arrived by Supply Col at 08.00. Refilled at once and delivered to Units. Company moved at 12.15 and arrived VOORMIEZEELE 14.30. TH/18676 / CPL ELLARD H.J. mounted Gas from 15.7.1918. Weather fine and rain at night.	
28/H 36 L.S.H	2.10.18		Rations drawn from Supply Col 08.00 refilled - delivered to units. T3/027805 Dr PARKER W returned from leave. Weather fine	L.T
	3.10.18		T4/124958 WAR CPL WALKER S.G. proceeded on leave to U.K.	L.T
	4.10.18		Rations drawn from Supply Col 08.00 and delivered in above. Weather fine	L.T
			Company moved at 10.30 to CAFE' BELGE. Weather fine	L.T
28/H 24 C3.2	5.10.18		Rations on usual T86/307 Cpl GREEN F proceeded on leave to U.K. Weather wet	L.T
			SH/070792 PTE BRADBURY H returned from leave.	
	6.10.18		Rations as usual. Company moved by road at 12.00 arrived in new camp near POPERINGHE W. 14.30. Dr SS. COOK TH proceeded on leave to the U.K. T7/07635 Dr YARDLEY F.J. returned from leave. Weather fine	L.T
28/G 9 L.9.8	7.10.18		Rations arrived by Supply Col at 07.30. Refilled at 09.00 and delivered to Units. T3/027102 Dr HUNTER B proceeded on leave to U.K. Weather fine	L.T

Army Form C. 2118.

WAR DIARY
or
INTELLIGENCE SUMMARY.
(Erase heading not required.)

Instructions regarding War Diaries and Intelligence Summaries are contained in F. S. Regs., Part II. and the Staff Manual respectively. Title pages will be prepared in manuscript.

Place	Date	Hour	Summary of Events and Information	Remarks and references to Appendices
28/G.19 d.g.5.	8.10.18		Rations moved by Supply Col at 07.30 and delivered to Unit. 09.30 Weather fine	L.T.
"	9.10.18		Rations as above. Rations delivered at 10.30. T304906 Dr BRADBURY W.T. returned from Base. Weather fine	L.T.
"	10.10.18		Rations arrived at 07.30 by Supply Col. Dump at 10.00 S=RGT 34 09071 Weather fine	L.T.
"	11.10.18		STEWART A. proceeded on leave to U.K. Rations as above. Supply Section left in afternoon for new camp. Weather fine	L.T.
"	12.10.18		Company left by road at 07.30 for new camp, arrived 10.30. Ration drawn from Railhead at 09.30. Dump at 10.00 refilled & delivered T.058575 Cpl BOLTON J.J. and 207792 Pte DISLEY L. returned from leave. Weather dull, some rain	L.T.
2S/H24.d.7.9	13.10.18		T.36754 Dr DODSON W. proceeded on leave to the U.K. Rations delivered by Supply Col at 08.30 refilled & delivered. Weather Rain all day	L.T.
"	14.10.18		Rations drawn from Railhead (TROIS ROIS) by H.T. 07.30. Refilled and delivered to Unit. Weather fine	L.T.
"	15.10.18		Rations drawn from Railhead as above refilled delivered. Weather fine	L.T.
"	16.10.18		Dump at 07.30 refilled & delivered. Company moved by road at 09.45 for new camp at DADIZEELE arrived 14.30. Tu.28 W.18 c 09. Weather wet.	L.T.

Army Form C. 2118.

WAR DIARY
or
INTELLIGENCE SUMMARY.
(Erase heading not required.)

Place	Date	Hour	Summary of Events and Information	Remarks and references to Appendices
DADIZEELE Sheet 28 N.9.c.6.04	17.10.18		Ration drawn from Supply Col at 10.30. Refilled & delivered to Units. T4057350 Dr Young J.M. proceeded on leave to U.K. Weather fine	G.T.
	18.10.18		Supply Col delivered ration again at 20.30. Refilled at 08.30 and delivered to Units. Ration received by from Supply Col at 12.00. Dumped & refilled at 14.00. Weather fine	G.T.
	19.10.18		Routine on form the 1st 75.8951 Sad Cpl Jobson T proceeded on leave to the U.K. Weather fine	G.T.
29/G.20.C.2.0	20.10.18		Ration left for units at 11.45. Ration received from Supply Col at new dump refilled 16.00. Company proceeded by road at 13.30 for new camp at Gulleghem arrived 15.30. Weather very dull but fine	G.T.
"	21.10.18		Rations delivered to units at 08.15. Company moved by road for new camp at Bisseghem at 13.30 arrived 14.15. Rations delivered by Supply Col at 15.30 dumped refilled at 16.00. Rain in morning dull but fine rest of day	G.T.
29/G.29.C.6.6	22.10.18		Rations delivered to Units at 08.15. Ration received from Supply Col 13.00 arrived 20.00. Weather fine	G.T.
"	23.10.18		Dump at 07.45 refilled & delivered to Units. Ration drawn from Supply Col at 15.00 refilled at 15.30. Weather fine	G.T.

WAR DIARY
or
INTELLIGENCE SUMMARY.
(Erase heading not required.)

Army Form C. 2118.

Place	Date	Hour	Summary of Events and Information	Remarks and references to Appendices
29/G 29 C.6.5.	24.10.18		Return delivered to Units at 08.15. Dump refill at 17.30. Weather fine	L.T.
"	25.10.18		Return delivered to Units at 07.45. No dump to refill. Weather fine	L.T.
"	26.10.18		Rations received from Supply fort at 06.00 dumped refilled at 07.15 and delivered to Units. Supply fort again delivered ration at 23.00. Weather fine	L.T.
"	27.10.18		Dump't refill and delivered ration to Units at 07.00. Return drawn by H.T. from Railhead LEDGHEM at 15.00. Weather fine	L.T.
"	28.10.18		Routine as for 27th. Weather, sunny & warm	L.T.
"	29.10.18		Routine as for 28. Supplies drawn from BISSEGHEM at 17.00. Company moved by road at 13.45 for COURTRAI arrived 15.20. 632786 Pte HARTLEY. P joined for duty from 238 Employment Co. H/21562 Dr JENNS A joined from 131 H.T.D. and transferred for duty with 138 FIELD AMBULANCE	L.T.
29/H32 d.9.2	30.10.18		Dump + refill at 09.00. Ration drawn from BISSEGHEIM Railhead at 15.15. Weather fine	L.T.
"	31.10.18		Routine as for 30th. Weather fine	L.T.

O.C. No. 2 COY. 41st DIVISIONAL TRAIN

Army Form C. 2118.

WAR DIARY
or
INTELLIGENCE SUMMARY.
(Erase heading not required.)

Instructions regarding War Diaries and Intelligence Summaries are contained in F. S. Regs., Part II. and the Staff Manual respectively. Title pages will be prepared in manuscript.

Place	Date	Hour	Summary of Events and Information	Remarks and references to Appendices
29/H32d9x	1-11-18		Dump refilled at 09.00. Ration drawn from BISSEGHEM railhead at 19.30.	16.7
			Lt R.W. MAYSON + CAPT MORRIS admitted to 140th Field Ambulance. Weather fine	
"	2-11-18		Dump refilled + delivered to units. 08:30. Ration drawn from railhead at 17:15.	16.7
			T/235830 Dr HALL S proceeded on leave 15 U.K. Company moved at 10-30	
			to SNEVEGHEM arrived 11.40. Weather still fine	
29/N6 a 2 b	3-11-18		Dump refilled & delivered 09.00. Ration drawn from railhead at 13.30	16.7
				Weather fine
"	4-11-18		Dump refilled & delivered to unit at 08.00. Ration drawn from railhead at 10-50 and dumped at	16.7
			BISSEGHEM at 13.45. Company moved at Weather fine	
			new camp 12.15. DEERLIJK STATION	
126.A.10.0 29/I32&4p4	5-11-18		Dumped refilled & delivered to unit at 08.30. Ration drawn from	16.7
			railhead at 14.00. CAPT MORRIS reported to from Hospital Weather very wet	
"	6-11-18		Dump refilled & delivered to unit. 08.45. Ration drawn from railhead	16.7
			at 14.00. Weather very wet	
"	7-11-18		Supply vehicles on for 6th Company moved at 12.25 for new camp, by	16.7
			road arrived DEERLIJK VILLAGE 13.35 Weather very wet	
			T/140033 Pr R. BALL 15 admitted to 140th Field Amb.	

WAR DIARY
or
INTELLIGENCE SUMMARY.

(Erase heading not required.)

Army Form C. 2118.

Place	Date	Hour	Summary of Events and Information	Remarks and references to Appendices
2/J3 c 3.6.	8.11.18		Dumps refilled, delivered to Unit 08.45. Ration drawn from Supply Col at 14.30 dumped refilled 15.00. Weather wet.	Lt J
"	9.11.18		Ration drawn from VICHTE refilled at 10.30. Weather fine	Lt J
"	10.11.18	07.00	Dumps a refilled and delivered to Unit. Ration drawn from Supply Col dumped refilled at 17.00. Company moved at 10.30 by road arrived new camp at 13.00 KLEINBERG. Weather fine	Lt J
29/J34.00	11.11.18	06.00	Ration delivered to units at 06.00. Ration drawn from Supply Col & Dumped. Company moved by road at 12.45 arrived at BERCHEM at 14.30. Weather fine	Lt J
"	12.11.18		Refilled delivered to Units at 08.30. Ration received from Supply Col 13.00 and dumped. 34/656882 Pte Smith HT left for leave to UK. Weather fine	Lt J
"	13.11.18		Refilled at 08.30 & delivered to Units. Weather fine	Lt J
30/N72.9	14.11.18	08.30	Company moved at 08.30, arrived at NEDERBRAKEL at 15.15 TS/7533 Dr WHR POWELL proceeded on leave to UK. Ration received from Supply Col and dumped. Weather fine	Lt J
"	15.11.18	09.00	Refilled delivered ration to Unit at 09.00. Ration received from Supply Col & dumped. Weather fine	Lt J

Army Form C. 2118

WAR DIARY
or
INTELLIGENCE SUMMARY
(Erase heading not required.)

Place	Date	Hour	Summary of Events and Information	Remarks and references to Appendices
30/N17a.1.9	16.11.18		Routine as for Nov 15th T/13119 S.S.M Eycott F T/057304 Dr ARNOLD A proceeded on leave to U.K. Weather frosty & fine	C.T.
"	17.11.18		Routine as usual. T/23972 Dr COCKBURN T proceeded on leave to the U.K. also S4/146290 Serg' GOODMAN A. Refieed. Weather frosty fine	C.T.
"	18.11.18	16.00	Company moved by road at 08.45 for VIANE, arrived at 13.00	C.T.
30/V24.C.3.3	19.11.18		Ration received from Supply Col and dumped. Weather frosty fine	C.T.
"	20.11.18		Refilled and delivered ration trunk at 09.00. Weather wet & cold	C.T.
"			Company moved at 09.45 by road for EVERBECQ arrived 12.45 Ration delivered to trunk at 14.00. Ration received from Supply Col at 21.00 Weather wet	C.T.
30/V2.d.4.4	21.11.18		T/284840 Dr Cox J admitted to 138th Fd Amb. Refilled delivered to trunk at 09.00 Weather frosty & fine	C.T.
"	22.11.18		Ration received from Supply Col at 02.00. Refilled delivered to trunk at 09.00 Weather frosty & fine	C.T.
"	23.11.18		Ration received from Supply Col 04.00. Refilled delivered to trunk at 09.00 Weather frosty & fine	C.T.
"	24.11.18		Ration received from Supply Col 02.30. Routine as usual Weather frosty & fine	C.T.

Army Form C. 2118.

WAR DIARY
or
INTELLIGENCE SUMMARY.
(Erase heading not required.)

Instructions regarding War Diaries and Intelligence Summaries are contained in F.S. Regs., Part II. and the Staff Manual respectively. Title pages will be prepared in manuscript.

Place	Date	Hour	Summary of Events and Information	Remarks and references to Appendices
30/UD d.44	25-11-18		Rations received from Suffly Col at 0830. Refilled & delivered to Unit at 09.00. Weather wet	G.T.
			T/124953 WHR CPL WALKER S.G. admitted to 138 Field Amb	G.T.
			Ration received from Suffly Col again at 23.00	G.T.
"	26.11.918		Routine as usual. Weather fine	G.T.
			T/307033 Dr JOHNSON H. T/065298 Dr COTTON F. proceeded	G.T.
"	27.11.918		on leave to the U.K. Weather fine	G.T.
"	28.11.918		Routine as usual. Weather fine	G.T.
"	29.11.918		Routine as usual. C.O. inspected first line transport. T/057534 Dr McNAMA O proceeded on leave to the Uh Kingdom. Weather fine	G.T.
"	30.11.918		Routine as usual. Weather fine	G.T.

CAPTAIN,
O.C., No. 2 COY, 41st DIVISIONAL TRAIN

Army Form C. 2118.

WAR DIARY
OR
INTELLIGENCE SUMMARY.
(Erase heading not required.)

I. No 2 Company H.T. Kirkcudbrightian

Place	Date	Hour	Summary of Events and Information	Remarks and references to Appendices
EVERBECQ	30/1/2.4.4			
	1.12.18		Rifles & delivered to Unit at 09.00 T30.9239 DR CLIFF I.E. proceeded on leave to the United Kingdom	26.J.
	2.12.18		Routine as usual. Weather fine	16.J
	3.12.18		Routine as usual T/22336 Cpl CHIDGAY H special leave to the United Kingdom. Weather fine	16.J
	4.12.18		Routine as usual 2nd Lt MAYSON R.W. reported from hospital. Weather wet-	16.J
"	5.12.18		Routine as usual. Weather wet-	16.J
"	6.12.18		Routine as usual. Weather dull	16.J
"	7.12.18		Routine as usual CAPT TRIPP proceeded on leave to UK. Weather fine	16.J
"	8.12.18		Routine as usual 2nd Lt CRAFTIER F.W. 12/13 Batt SURREY Regt attached for instructional purposes. Weather very fine & sunny	16.J
"	9.12.18		Routine as usual. Weather fine	16.J
"	10.12.18		Routine as usual. Weather wet-	16.J
"	11.12.18		Routine as usual 11th Bgde RFA wagon left for 16°. Weather wet-	16.J
"	12.12.18		T/263853 DR HALL A T/265734 DR BROWN A.W. joined from 13.A.T.D	16.J
"	13.12.18		Company moved by road at 07.30 to TEMBROEK area, arrived 14.15. Dumped & refilled. Weather very wet-	16.J

WAR DIARY
or
INTELLIGENCE SUMMARY.
(Erase heading not required.)

Army Form C. 2118.

Place	Date	Hour	Summary of Events and Information	Remarks and references to Appendices
TEMBROEK	13/7/18		Return received at 24.00. Company moved by road from TEMBROEK at 10.30 arrived SAINTES 13.00	
SAINTES	14/7/18		Refilled delivered at 07.30 delivered. Company moved by road arrived at WAUTHIER CHATEAU at 11.30. Return received at 22.30. Bgde CATLIN proceeded on leave to U.K. Weather fine	
WAUTHIER CHATEAU	15/7/18		Refilled delivered at 09.00. Sergt COVEY proceeded on leave to the United Kingdom. Weather fine	
"	16/7/18		Return received from Supply last at 03.00, dumper refilled at 09.00. Company moved at 10.30 arrived at PLANCENOIT at 14.45. Weather wet.	
PLANCENOIT	17/7/18		Return received at 05.00 from Supply. Col dumpers refilled at 09.00. Company moved at 09.04 by road arrived RIGENEE at 13.30. Weather fine	
RIGENEE	18/7/18		Company moved at 11.00 by road arrived SOMBREFFE at 14.30. Return received from Supply Col dumpers & refilled at 16.30. CSM SCARRATT F proceeded on leave to U.K. Weather wet.	
SOMBREFFE	19/7/18		Return received at 01.00 refilled at 08.00 Company moved at 09.00 arrived SOMBREFFE at 13.00. Weather being fine	

Army Form C. 2118.

WAR DIARY
or
INTELLIGENCE SUMMARY.
(Erase heading not required.)

Place	Date	Hour	Summary of Events and Information	Remarks and references to Appendices
SUHRLEE	20/12/18	08.30	Returns rec'd at 08.30. Refilled at 09.00. Company marched to OTREPPE arriving at 14.00. Weather very bad with heavy rain storms. C.Q.M.S. pension presented a/c b VIX	b.i. b.VIX
OTREPPE	21/12/18		Company moved to Villers le Bouillet starting at 08.30. Returns were taken by the new billetin in lorries. Refilled at 15.00. Weather fine	b.i.
VILLERS LE BOUILLET	22/12/18		Company moved to Chausee de Straet, HUY at 9.30. Supply Officer & personnel remaining at VILLERS LE BOUILLET & functioning there	b.i.
HUY	23/12/18		Returns received at Refilled at 06.30. Refilled at 07.30 & both returned to Dumps at VILLERS LE BOUILLET. Weather stormy & cold	b.i.
"	24/12/18		Routine as above	Weather fine
"	25/12/18		Xmas Day. No parade.	Weather fine
"	26/12/18		Routine as usual. S/Sgt G. TRIPP left for leave to the following men having proceeded to England for demobilisation and obtained their demobilisation leave:-	b.i.
			T/4/014634 S/Sgt ARNOLD A. class ft	23.12.18
			T/4/105454 S/Sgt JOHNSTON R.	25.12.18
			T/4/039204 S/Sgt THOMAS S.	25.12.18
			T/4/054364 S/Sgt MILLER J.	26.12.18

WAR DIARY
or
INTELLIGENCE SUMMARY.

Army Form C. 2118.

(Erase heading not required.)

Place	Date	Hour	Summary of Events and Information	Remarks and references to Appendices
HQ	27/7/19		Routine as usual. Major C. TRIPP R.A.S.C. returned from leave U.K.	
			Weather fine	
"	28/7/19		Nothing to record	
"	29/7/19		Lieut. Hilton E. proceeded on leave to U.K. via Westwick	
			Men relieved by L.T. at 15.30 no one observed to jump L.M.D 13 & L.M.D 82 attempted	
			Low jump attained attempted.	
"	30/7/19		Guns laws dismissed at C.f. 30 guns observed to jump ineffectively	
"	31/7/19		Weather still Routine as usual	

A.V.H. Left
O/C 132 Company 41st Stationary [   ]

WAR DIARY
INTELLIGENCE SUMMARY

Army Form C. 2118

Place	Date	Hour	Summary of Events and Information	Remarks and references to Appendices
HUY LÉGE?	1/1/19		Sent by HT from Huy Station (NORD) at 04.30 ahead to stamp at VILLER'S LE BOULLER two return rations are drawn by first line transport 14/23/44 & SCOTT J.E. proceeds ahead have to I.R.	L.T.
"	2/1/19		Routine as usual. Weather dull	L.T.
"	3/1/19		Rations as usual. 9 O.R. rotated to duty from the base up by 98 "D" Coy from DUNBAR", two men proceeded overnight & through Rations on 2nd and 3rd O.R. rotated took two land rotation per	L.T.
"	4/1/19		Two rations by HT at 04.45 arrived to dump and drew again at 04.50 there rations arrived as above. 15 O.R. rotated for infantry Bn. for on march taken on Inspect Nubia No 15/9472 to Lee FURNIVAL S.C. from Pam Bambeft and bombers Lt 138 Suttle on absence study 12/9621 Lt ELLIS.R. and 14/08634 Lt EAST.J. joined from His Bn. of. Lt Capt. H.MORRIS RA's & Municipal from transfer and taken on the strength. 30.12.18 London Gazette.	No.1 Weather dull
"	5/1/19		Drew red rations at 04.00 and drew two Railwa at 11.30	L.T. Weather dull
"	6/1/19		Rations as usual. 1 O.R. returned from leave.	L.T.

WAR DIARY or INTELLIGENCE SUMMARY

Army Form C. 2118.

Place	Date	Hour	Summary of Events and Information	Remarks and references to Appendices
HUY LIÈGE 1	7th/19		Left ANTWERP at 08.15 from AMPSIN. Baggage arrived 10.15th Hants & Huy. Advance B.H.Q. Left moving Brig. entrained. Billeted Hants 13B. Fuller ambulance and Bn. B.H.Q. at HUY. Fallen in evening. Weather fine	L.J.
"	8th/19		Left ambulance as usual from AMPSIN. 1/c 2/B/1535 to 18th KRRC 2 day in evening at Bn. H.Q. 1c/y. Billet 22B to 18th KRRC & 2 day in evening at HUY. Weather fine 11/31535. O/c A. Wrench 74 I how 4 am. left & arrived through HUY NORD at 10.00 for GERMANY with 22B Field 109 RE Train etc. Weather wet.	L.J.
"	9th/19		Arrived at HUY at 11.59.	L.J.
SCHARREN- BROICH (RÖSRATH) near 2. GERMANY	10th/19		Entrained at WAHN at 5.30 had breakfast at station and moved off for camp at RÖSRATH at 7.5. Arrived at camp 11.30. Rations delivered. Bn. lorries 16 - 12 at boat on appr. 7.15th Hants. Rations delivered at camp. 16 Bn KRRC B.H.Q. & the Coy. 13B Fuller Amb. & 22B Field Coy RE Train. Weather fine	L.J.
"	11/19		Church parade to B.A.Q. & 18th KRRC were ordered at 9.0. New rations. Weather fine.	L.J.
"	12/19		Bn HT at 13.00 from RÖSRATH Pavilion. Church service. 15.0 H. Luards forming up of transport & horses 16.00 at EAST J transport at 16.5. 22 Svy 13th H.Q. Weather fine	L.J.

WAR DIARY
or
INTELLIGENCE SUMMARY.
(Erase heading not required.)

Army Form C. 2118.

Place	Date	Hour	Summary of Events and Information	Remarks and references to Appendices
SCHARREN-BROICH BOSRATH Nr 22 GERMANY	13/7/19		Educational training as usual. Lectures on M.T. & Infantry Formations	
			R'veil at 1330. Two wagons from 19th Middlesex Reported arrived at 1300	G.1
			Weather wet	
	14/7/19		Educational training as usual. Draw from R'head 19.30 5 or B.N.B. Lancasters.	G.V.
			Act relieved for escort from Infantry H'qtrs & sent to stn. n/s 5/35 5935 Pte CARPENTER No gloves	
				G.V.
	15/7/19		Educational training as usual. Cleaned at 11.30 and Rifle Inspection still going on. Weather fine	
	16/7/19		Routine as usual	G.V.
	17/7/19		Routine as usual Weather fine	G.V.
	18/7/19		Routine as usual 5/10689 L/Cpl Y/5/M F. SCARRATT awarded 7 days F.P.No.1 Weather still warm	G.V.
	19/7/19		Routine as usual Drew from R'head at 1130 Weather dull	G.V.
	20/7/19		Routine as usual 14/12494 53104 L/Cpl WALKER SG. Awarded 3 days F.P.No.2	
			Beaufort M.S. in a.m. in the afternoon Routine	
	21/7/19		Routine as usual Drew rations at 16.30 72/9621 to M.Y. C.C.S. and in the rest of weather find	G.V.
			Lecture on M.T. used	
	22/7/19		Routine as usual. Two days Rue rations and change over motions of weather cool	G.V.
			Wire Pulled at 10 mts	

WAR DIARY
or
INTELLIGENCE SUMMARY.
(Erase heading not required.)

Army Form C. 2118.

Instructions regarding War Diaries and Intelligence Summaries are contained in F. S. Regs., Part II. and the Staff Manual respectively. Title pages will be prepared in manuscript.

Place	Date	Hour	Summary of Events and Information	Remarks and references to Appendices
SCHARREN-BROICH RASRATH	23/7/19		Awaiting orders	
2cl 2 "	24/7/19		Awaiting orders	G.T.
"	25/7/19		Awaiting orders	
GERMANY	26/7/19		Received T/36541 Lt DAVIES R.W. being on secondment to the 24th Indian Divisional Train. Weather cold & dull	
	27/7/19		Rations sent out near from Railhead Werkhoeven G.T. dull	G.T.
			Provisions by lorries from HUMAR delivered rations with lorries	
	28/7/19		Received by H.T. from HUMAR at Dunkirk and drilled at 12 noon Weather fine	G.T.
	29/7/19		Rations from HUMAR by H.T. at 8.15, Divisional and supplies at 11.30 Weather fine	G.T.
	30/7/19		Rations arrived on head awful drilled. Draw rations from Railroad at 2.45 am	G.T.
	31/7/19		Drilled at 9.30 noon and drew rations from hour at 12.30 Weather better	G.T.
			Rail MORRIS RASC had been on sick list admitted slightly better	G.T.

WAR DIARY or INTELLIGENCE SUMMARY

Army Form C. 2118.

2 Company
1st Armenian

(Erase heading not required.)

Instructions regarding War Diaries and Intelligence Summaries are contained in F. S. Regs., Part II. and the Staff Manual respectively. Title pages will be prepared in manuscript.

Place	Date	Hour	Summary of Events and Information	Remarks and references to Appendices
SCHARREN-BRUCH (Raststatt) (GERMANY)	1/2/19		Distilled gas and other chloric actions	
"	2/2/19		CAPTAIN H MORRIS R.A.S.C. arrived to U.R. 31.1.19 to administer and stand at 14 HHHH 51 with DIBBEN C. proceed to 1 R. the day to remit mater and atoms up	L.T.
"	3/2/19		Arrived at 8.45 and drew from R'hurst at 10.30. Weather total standstill	L.T.
"	4/2/19		Rations as usual. arrived at 15.00. Weather total standstill	L.T.
			Lost orders for last lorries. 13th Hants 228 bgr 128 Brade DFA by H.T. 16 HUMAR by 04.45 for unloading and delivery by tram. Drivers no rest at U.B.D. Lime C.R. unloaded on tram. Weather foul	L.T.
"	5/2/19		Rations as usual. No.1.5/4948 Wh. Staff Sgt OATEN A.C. evacuated to C.C.S. and struck off. Weather standstill	L.T.
"	6/2/19		Rations as usual. 1/20336 Pte. Saff. gr PULLEN. Hospitalised on 3/1/- Weather frost to later	L.T.
"	7/2/19		Rations as usual. Whole company hauling 6-12 hours and wagons taken at HUMAR at 14.00 to Jagdby L.S.T. 2 wagons. Weather tea very cold	L.T.
"	8/2/19		Rations as usual. Weather very cold	L.T.

WAR DIARY
or
INTELLIGENCE SUMMARY.
(Erase heading not required.)

Army Form C. 2118.

Place	Date	Hour	Summary of Events and Information	Remarks and references to Appendices
SCHARREN-BROICH ROSRATH Bez Cs GERMANY	10/7/19		Routine as usual. 1OR returned from leave	
	11/7/19		Routine as usual. Weather fine cloudy	
			Weather fine. 2 LCols	
	12/7/19		Routine as usual. 20 F PICKFORD attached on Prob. Weather fine	
			Extra work at ROSRATH BHF for unit proceeding to Germany rations for HUMAR	
			returning from leave. 1OR Luxurian leave. 2 WC RW MAYSON	
			7/32494 Cpl LUNTLEY GW & T/M 1126 L/Cpl PUGH AC joined	
			for duty on mobilization from 139 Guelm Ambulance. 6 th new F. R. M.	
	13/7/19		Routine as usual. 14/065215 R/21226 HURST RJ reported to C C S on 11 th	
			and struck off. Weather fine	
	14/7/19		Routine as usual. 14/059340 Pte YOUNG J M reported to CCS on	
			11 th and so struck off. Weather fine	
	15/7/19		Routine as usual. 1OR returned from leave. Weather warm & dull	
	16/7/19		Routine as usual. Weather previous	
	17/7/19		Routine as usual. Weather wet	
	18/7/19		Routine as usual. 4 OR with full Christian brethren from	
	19/7/19		Routine as usual. Weather fine	

Army Form C. 2118.

WAR DIARY
or
INTELLIGENCE SUMMARY.
(Erase heading not required.)

Instructions regarding War Diaries and Intelligence Summaries are contained in F. S. Regs., Part II. and the Staff Manual respectively. Title pages will be prepared in manuscript.

Place	Date	Hour	Summary of Events and Information	Remarks and references to Appendices
SCHARREN-BROICH ROSRATH	20/7/19		Routine as usual. 10R proceeded on leave. Weather fine	L.J.
Ditto	21/7/19		Routine as usual. 10R proceeded on leave. Weather fine	L.J.
GERMANY	22/7/19		Routine as usual. 14/105/390 L. YOUNG J. M. proceeded on 20th inst. from CCS and taken on strength from 20th. 14/1065318 a/L/Cpl HURST R.J. rejoined from CCS on 21st and taken on strength. SER. Weather chang.	L.J.
	23/7/19		Routine as usual. 30R proceeded on leave. Weather dull	L.J.
	24/7/19		Routine as usual. Weather fine	L.J.
	25/7/19		Routine as usual. Weather wet	L.J.
	26/7/19		Routine as usual. 30R proceeded on leave. Draw proceeding ourwords. Weather hot	L.J.
	27/7/19		Routine as usual. 18th A.R.R.C. Lieut. the Baron 14/9th Rebelliam joined the stream S3658 5 Pte CARPENTER M.H. evacuated to C.S. arrival 15 C.C.S. no 232/4	L.J.
	28/7/19		Routine as usual. 1 Meat stolen	L.J.
	29/7/19		Routine as usual. Weather dull	L.J.

G. Toll
CAPTAIN,
O.C. No. 2 COY. 41st DIVISIONAL TRAIN

2nd z GERMANY

Army Form C. 2118.

WAR DIARY
or
INTELLIGENCE SUMMARY
(Erase heading not required.)

Instructions regarding War Diaries and Intelligence Summaries are contained in F. S. Regs., Part II. and the Staff Manual respectively. Title pages will be prepared in manuscript.

Place	Date	Hour	Summary of Events and Information	Remarks and references to Appendices
SCHARREN-BROICH ROSRATH	1 3/19		Routine as usual. 74/23441 Sgt SCOTT J.E having been granted extra	6.7
	2 3/19		on leave to attend the boys H.A to Jan 19. Weather fine	
			Sgt from HOMAR to H.I at 11.30 am yesterday allowed to return to by	6.7
			train at 8.15 hours 2 and H.I at 09.00. Weather fine	
	3 3/19		Routine as usual. 2nd Lieut PICKFORD W.F returned from leave. Routine fine	6.7
	4 3/19		Routine as usual. 1 O.R. returned from leave. Weather wet	6.7
	5 3/19		Routine as usual. Weather fine	6.7
	6 3/19		Routine as usual. 54/035658 dept. WINKLEY A.E. having trained &	6.7
			employed for investigation in ranch off 1 H.D. and 1 train intelligence in 6th inst, was	
			struck off. Weather wet	
	7 3/19		Routine as usual. 2 O.R. proceeded on leave to U.K. Weather fine	6.7
	8 3/19		Sgt from Rhead at noon time and arrived at 11.30 am. Weather fine	6.7
	9 3/19		Routine as usual. Weather fine	6.7
	10 3/19		Routine as usual. 54/124953 A/L/cpl WALKER S.G evacuated to	6.7
			4th mil. and struck off the strength. 1 O.R proceeded on leave to UK.	
	11 3/19		Routine as usual. 1 O.R returned from leave. Weather fine	6.7

WAR DIARY
or
INTELLIGENCE SUMMARY

Army Form C. 2118.

Part 2 GERMANY

Place	Date	Hour	Summary of Events and Information	Remarks and references to Appendices
SCHARREN-BROICH ROSRATH	12/3/19		Routine as usual. 1/2nd Lieut W.F. PICKFORD appointed acting Lieut on 12.2	B.T.
			Intensity Barrack	
	13/3/19		Routine as usual. 1 R relieved 11 Hvy Bde & gave leave of 30 O.R.	
			Hvy Bty 2.30 p.m. Lieut Ld & Sterling relieved by the remainder 10 R	G.T.
			Lung to war with machine tractors	
				Routine as usual	Weather fine
	14/3/19		Routine as usual	Weather fine	16.3.?
	15/3/19		Routine as usual	Weather fine	20.3.?
	16/3/19		Routine as usual	Weather fine	16.3.?
	17/3/19		Routine as usual. 100 O.R. returned from leave	Weather low temperature	16.3.?
	18/3/19		Routine as usual. 10 R proceeded on leave	Weather cold & chill	16.3.?
	19/3/19		Routine as usual	Weather fine & cold	W.H.P.
	20/3/19		Routine as usual. Capt. TRIPP left for Paris (leave)	Weather fine	W.H.P.
	21/3/19		Routine as usual	Weather cold & dull	W.H.P.
	22/3/19		Routine as usual. 1/9th 6 Surveys took over outpost line	Weather fine	W.H.P.
	23/3/19		Routine as usual	Weather mild	W.H.P.
	24/3/19		Routine as usual. 10 R ret'd from leave	Weather fine	W.H.P.

WAR DIARY
or
INTELLIGENCE SUMMARY
(Erase heading not required.)

Army Form C. 2118.

Place	Date	Hour	Summary of Events and Information	Remarks and references to Appendices
SCHARRENBROICH				
ROSRATH	25/3		Routine as usual. C.Q.M.S. Johnson struck off strength from 12/3	WSP
	26/3		Routine as usual. 1 O.R. ret'd from leave.	WSP
	27/3		Routine as usual	WSP
	28/3		Routine as usual. B.1 & 13 "Y" R.F.A. relieved A.1 & B.44 A.F.A. 1 O.R. ret'd from leave	WSP
	29/3		Routine as usual. CAPT TRIPP ret'd from PARIS LEAVE	WSP
	30/3		Routine as usual. 1 O.R. ret'd from leave	WSP
	31/3		Routine as usual	W.I.T

Weather fine + cold
Weather cold + sunny
Weather cold but fine
Weather dull + sunny
Weather sunny + cold
Weather snowy + cold
Weather cold + dull

CAPTAIN,
D.C. No. 2 COY. DIVISIONAL TRAIN
LONDON

WAR DIARY or INTELLIGENCE SUMMARY

Army Form C. 2118.

[handwritten header, partially legible: "...L GERMANY   Day ...   London Br train"]

Place	Date	Hour	Summary of Events and Information	Remarks and references to Appendices
SCHARREN-BROICH ROSRATH	1/7/19		Sent a convoy from H.Q. MAR. Rothead by H.T. arrived Hilliers at 11.30 & C R returned from base on 31st inst.	L.T.
	2/7/19		Routine as usual. March part two standard of 8th boat troop arr 1/7 Weather fine	L.T.
	3/7/19		[illegible] annual medical Insp? Capt of 2/8 ? arrived at 23 ? invalided out	L.T.
			[illegible] 2nd Lt Goodman & worked to M.H.C.C.S on return ? ? ?	L.T.
	4/7/19		[illegible] Weather fine	L.T.
	5/7/19		Routine as usual. 3 H.D horses came from 1st S.R.Cy train to T4/06 C.2118	L.T.
			2/Lt HURST appointed t/Lt from 6.4.18 Weather fine	
	6/7/19		Routine as usual over M.H.D x horses in exchange for first H.D.2 horses. Weather fine	L.T.
	7/7/19		Routine as usual. T4/124593 Wkr L/Cpl WALKER R.S.C. Weather fine	L.T.
	8/7/19		Leave granted from M.H.C.C.S. on 4-hour no ? ? ? Routine as usual.	L.T.
				Weather dull and warmer
	9/7/19		Routine as usual. Weather fine	L.T.
	10/7/19		Routine as usual. Inspected B Coy m.y.C. Lamport Weather fine	L.T.

WAR DIARY
or
INTELLIGENCE SUMMARY.
(Erase heading not required.)

Army Form C. 2118.

Instructions regarding War Diaries and Intelligence Summaries are contained in F. S. Regs., Part II. and the Staff Manual respectively. Title pages will be prepared in manuscript.

Place	Date	Hour	Summary of Events and Information	Remarks and references to Appendices
SCHARREN BROICH	11/4/19		Routine as usual	WSP
	12/4/19		Routine as usual. Cap? Tutp handed over Company on being sent to England for Demobilisation. t was struck off strength from this date.	WSP
	13/4/19		Routine as usual. Weather mild & wet	WSP
	14/4/19		Routine as usual. Weather fine & windy	WSP
	15/4/19		Routine as usual. Weather fine	WSP
	16/4/19		Routine as usual. 1.O.R. returned from leave. Weather fair & cold	WSP
	17/4/19		Routine as usual. Weather fine	WSP
	18/4/19		Routine as usual. Delivered rations twice by Rail. Weather fine	WSP
	19/4/19		Routine as usual. Weather fine	WSP
	20/4/19		Routine as usual. 1.O.R. ret? from leave. Weather fine	WSP
	21/4/19		Routine as usual. Weather sunny	WSP
	22/4/19		Routine as usual. Weather cold	WSP
	23/4/19		Routine as usual. Weather fine + cold	WSP
	24/4/19		Routine as usual. Weather stormy	WSP
	25/4/19		Routine as usual. G.O.C inspected the Company. Weather cold with hail	WSP

Army Form C. 2118.

WAR DIARY
or
INTELLIGENCE SUMMARY.
(Erase heading not required.)

Place	Date	Hour	Summary of Events and Information	Remarks and references to Appendices
SCHARRENBROICH	26/7/19		Routine as usual. Weather stormy + cold	WRP
ROSRATH	27/7/19		Routine as usual. Weather stormy + cold	WRP
	28/7/19		Routine as usual. Div¹ Race Meeting 1st day. Weather fine + cold	WRP
	29/7/19		Routine as usual. Div¹ Race Meeting 2nd day. Weather fine + cold	WRP
	30/7/19		Routine as usual. Weather fine	WRP

W.P. Pickford
CAPTAIN
O.C. No. 2 COY 2d DIVISIONAL TRAIN

WAR DIARY
or
INTELLIGENCE SUMMARY. No 2 Coy/Jordan Bn. Train

(Erase heading not required.)

Army Form C. 2118.

Place	Date	Hour	Summary of Events and Information	Remarks and references to Appendices
SCHARREN-BROICH nr Rosrath.	1/5/19		Routine as usual. Weather snowy	WDP
	2/5/19		" " " Weather cold	WDP
	3/5/19		Routine as usual. Weather dull	WDP
	4/5/19		Routine as usual Weather fine	WDP
	5/5/19		Routine as usual Weather fine	WDP
	6/5/19		Routine as usual Weather fine	WDP
	7/5/19		Routine as usual Weather fine	WDP
	8/5/19		Routine as usual Weather wet	WDP
	9/5/19		Routine as usual Weather fine	WDP
	10/5/19		Routine as usual Weather warm	WDP
	11/5/19		Routine as usual Weather fine	WDP
	12/5/19		Routine as usual. 1st London Bde went back to Reserve Area Weather fine	WDP
	13/5/19		Routine as usual Coy moved to Heumar + took over from No 4 Coy. Weather fine	WDP
HEUMAR	14/5/19		Routine as usual. Weather fine	WDP
	15/5/19		Routine as usual Weather fine	WDP
	16/5/19		Routine as usual Weather fine	WDP

Army Form C. 2118.

WAR DIARY
or
INTELLIGENCE SUMMARY. 2 Cav./ord. Du. Train

(Erase heading not required.)

Instructions regarding War Diaries and Intelligence Summaries are contained in F. S. Regs., Part II. and the Staff Manual respectively. Title pages will be prepared in manuscript.

Place	Date	Hour	Summary of Events and Information	Remarks and references to Appendices
HEUMAR	MAR 17/19		Routine as usual	WTP
	18/19		Routine as usual	WTP
	19/19		Routine as usual. Sent Pair of Huabaden 15 x 2" trench doors Showhorses & wagon	WTP
	20/19		Routine as usual	WTP
	21/19		Routine as usual	WTP
	22/19		Routine as usual	WTP
	23/19		Routine as usual	WTP
	24/19		Routine as usual	WTP
	25/19		Routine as usual	WTP
	26/19		Routine as usual	WTP
	27/19		Routine as usual	WTP
	28/19		Routine as usual	WTP
	29/19		Routine as usual	WTP
	30/19		Routine as usual	WTP
	31/19		Routine as usual	WTP

Weather fine (all dates)

WAR DIARY
or
INTELLIGENCE SUMMARY.
(Erase heading not required.)

Army Form C. 2118.

2 Coy London Div Army ...

Place	Date	Hour	Summary of Events and Information	Remarks and references to Appendices
HEUMAR	1/6/19		Routine as usual.	Weather fine
"	2/6/19		— do —	— do —
"	3/6/19		— do —	— do —
"	4/6/19		— do —	— do —
"	5/6/19		— do —	— do —
"	6/6/19		— do —	— do —
"	7/6/19		— do —	— do —
"	8/6/19		— do —	— do —
"	9/6/19		— do —	— do —
"	10/6/19		— do —	— do —
"	11/6/19		— do —	— do —
"	12/6/19		— do —	— do —
"	13/6/19		— do —	— do —
"	14/6/19		— do —	— do —
"	15/6/19		— do —	— do —
"	16/6/19		— do —	— do —

WAR DIARY
or
INTELLIGENCE SUMMARY. 2 Coy/Ridgr Div Train

Army Form C. 2118.

(Erase heading not required.)

Place	Date	Hour	Summary of Events and Information	Remarks and references to Appendices
HEUMAR	17/9		Routine as usual	Weather fine
"	18/9		— do —	— do —
"	19/9		Company moved by march Route 02-30 hours. Arrived VERATH 07-30 Hours	Weather fine
OVERATH	20/9		Routine as usual	— do —
"	21/9		— do —	— do —
"	22/9		— do —	Weather wet
"	23/9		— do —	— do —
"	24/9		— do —	— do —
"	25/9		— do —	— do —
"	26/9		— do —	— do —
"	27/9		— do —	— do —
"	28/9		— do —	— do —
"	29/9		— do —	— do —
"	30/9		Company moved by march Route 04-30 hours. Arrived HEUMAR 08-30 hours	

Army Form C. 2118.

WAR DIARY
or
INTELLIGENCE SUMMARY.
(Erase heading not required.)

2 Coy London Div Train

Place	Date	Hour	Summary of Events and Information	Remarks and references to Appendices
RATH HEUMAR	1/7/19		Routine as usual	Weather Dull
	2/7/19		-do-	" "
	3/7/19		-do-	" "
	4/7/19		-do-	" "
	5/7/19		-do-	" Showery
	6/7/19		-do-	" "
	7/7/19		-do-	" Dull
	8/7/19		-do-	" "
	9/7/19		-do-	" Showery
	10/7/19		-do-	" "
	11/7/19		-do-	" Dull
	12/7/19		-do-	" "
	13/7/19		-do-	" "
	14/7/19		-do-	" Showery
	15/7/19		-do-	" "
	16/7/19		-do-	" Dull

Sheet 2.

WAR DIARY
or
INTELLIGENCE SUMMARY.
(Erase heading not required.)

Army Form C. 2118.

2 Coy London Div Train

Place	Date	Hour	Summary of Events and Information	Remarks and references to Appendices
RATH HEUMAR	1/7/19		Routine as usual	Weather Showery
	2/7/19		- do -	" "
	3/7/19		- do -	" Dull
	19/7/19		- do -	" Showery
	20/7/19		- do -	" Dull
	21/7/19		- do -	" Showery
	22/7/19		- do -	" "
	23/7/19		- do -	" Dull
	24/7/19		- do -	" Dull
	25/7/19		- do -	" Showery
	26/7/19		- do -	" "
	27/7/19		- do -	" "
	28/7/19		- do - T/356239 Dr Williams proceeded on leave	" Dull
	29/7/19		- do -	" "
	30/7/19		- do -	" "
	31/7/19		- do -	" Fine

W Duff Lieut
OC No 2 Coy London Div Train

Army Form C. 2118.

WAR DIARY
or
INTELLIGENCE SUMMARY. H° 2 Coy London Div Train

(Erase heading not required.)

Instructions regarding War Diaries and Intelligence Summaries are contained in F. S. Regs., Part II. and the Staff Manual respectively. Title pages will be prepared in manuscript.

Place	Date	Hour	Summary of Events and Information	Remarks and references to Appendices
RATH HEUMAR	August 1919 1		Routine as usual	Weather fine
	2		do	"
	3		do	"
	4		do	"
	5		do	"
	6		do	"
	7		do	"
	8		do	"
	9		do	"
	10		do	"
	11		do	"
	12		do	"
	13		do	"
	14		do	"
	15		do	"
	16		do	"

Army Form C. 2118.

WAR DIARY
or
INTELLIGENCE SUMMARY.
(Erase heading not required.)

1 Coy/London Dis Train

Place	Date	Hour	Summary of Events and Information	Remarks and references to Appendices
Rall Heuvert	August 1919 17		Routine as Usual	
	18		do	Weather fine
	19		do	" "
	20		do	" "
	21		do	" "
	22		do	" "
	23		do	" "
	24		do	" "
	25		do	" "
	26		do	" "
	27		do	" "
	28		do	" "
	29		do	" "
	30		do	" "
	31		do	Weather showery

WAR DIARY No 397 Cy Labour Bn Army Form C. 2118.
or
INTELLIGENCE SUMMARY.
(Erase heading not required.)

Place	Date	Hour	Summary of Events and Information	Remarks and references to Appendices
Rath Henan	1/9/19		Routine as usual	Seven Line
"	2/9/19		do	" "
"	3/9/19		do	" "
"	4/9/19		do	" "
"	5/9/19		do	" "
"	6/9/19		do	" "
"	7/9/19		do	" "
"	8/9/19		do	" "
"	9/9/19		do	" "
"	10/9/19		do	" "
"	11/9/19		do	" "
"	12/9/19		do	" "
"	13/9/19		do	" "
"	14/9/19		do	" "
"	15/9/19		do	" "
"	16/9/19		do	" "

WAR DIARY 397 Coy/London Div. Train
or
INTELLIGENCE SUMMARY.
(Erase heading not required.)

Army Form C. 2118.

Instructions regarding War Diaries and Intelligence Summaries are contained in F. S. Regs., Part II. and the Staff Manual respectively. Title pages will be prepared in manuscript.

Place	Date	Hour	Summary of Events and Information	Remarks and references to Appendices
Ratt Newnan	1/9/19		Routine as usual	Weather fine
"	8/9/19		do	"
"	11/9/19		do	"
"	20/9/19		do	"
"	21/9/19		do	"
"	22/9/19		do	"
"	23/9/19		do	"
"	24/9/19		do	"
"	25/9/19		do	"
"	26/9/19		do	"
"	27/9/19		do	weather bad
"	28/9/19		do	weather fine
"	29/9/19		do	"

Eddy Lieut
O.C. 397 Coy R.A.S.C.
London Div. Train

WAR DIARY 297 Coy R.A.S.C.
or
INTELLIGENCE SUMMARY. London on War

Army Form C. 2118.

Place	Date	Hour	Summary of Events and Information	Remarks and references to Appendices
RATH HEUMAR			ROUTINE AS USUAL	

14.31.10.19

APPENDIX I

o/o 2 Coy, 41st Divisional Train

In the Field   Daily State

No. 2 COMPANY, 41st DIVISIONAL TRAIN

No. ....
Date: January 1st 1917

	Officers	W. Officers	W.O. 2nd cl.	C.Q.M.S.	Sergeants	Farriers	Saddlers	Wheelers	Artificers Drivers	Total	Riding	Horses H.Draught	Mules	Wagon G.S.	Vehicles W.Limber	Carts Water	Supply Details
Establishment	3	1	1		2	3	3	4	52	70	13	50	6	23	2	1	1 Officer
Strength	4	1		1	2	3	3	4	52	70	12	50	6	23	2	1	B 1 S. Sergt
Attached									2	2		4		2			1 Sergt
Total	4	1		1	2	3	3	4	54	72	12	54	6	25	2	1	c 3 Corporals
On {Company	3			1					21	25	6	36		18			6 Privates
duty {Attached									2	2		4		2			& Includes 3 Corpls
Sick {Hospital									*1	1							* 1 Corpl in hospital
{Quarters												3	1				x Includes 1 Corpl
Absent with leave	1			1						2							{1 Pte from 122nd M.G.
Company Employ		1			1	3	3	4	x16	28		2				1	{Coy as Cold Shoer.
Detached									5	5	2	2	5			1	
Available									9	9	6	9	1			1	
Total	4	1		1	2	3	3	4	54	72	12	54	6	25	2	1	

Detached

A { Includes 1 Cook at Train Hd Qrs
    { " 2 Drs in detention
    { " 2 " at Trench Warfare School

B. S. Sergt at Train Hd Qrs.

C. Includes 1 H.T. Corpl at Train Hd Qrs.

H D Galbraith Capt
O.C No 2 Coy
41st Div Train

www.ingramcontent.com/pod-product-compliance
Lightning Source LLC
Chambersburg PA
CBHW081541160426
43191CB00011B/1808